Hope you
enjoy the Book.
Mann H. Holt

D0926116

Est. 1869

150 YEARS A PIONEER

THE UNLIKELY STORY OF BAKER BOYER, WALLA WALLA, AND THE REGION

THOMAS P. SKEEN

WITH KELLY BLACK

Documentary Media

Seattle

150 YEARS A PIONEER

The Unlikely Story of Baker Boyer, Walla Walla, and the Region

Baker Boyer

www.bakerboyer.com

(509) 525-2000

(800) 234-7923

Produced and published by:

Documentary Media LLC

books@docbooks.com

www.documentarymedia.com

(206) 935-9292

First Edition

Printed in the USA

By Thomas P. Skeen, with Kelly Black

Additional writing: Linda Andrews

Baker Boyer Project Manager/Creative Director: Kelly Black

Editor: Judy Gouldthorpe

Book Design: Marilyn Esguerra

Production Assistants: Tori Smith, Edward Daschle

Editorial Director: Petyr Beck, Documentary Media LLC

ISBN: 978-1-933245-59-1

CONTENTS

FOREWORD

By Megan Clubb

Glancing through the pages of this book, you will find a collection of stories that illustrate 150 years of entrepreneurialism and collaboration between Baker Boyer and our community—a true celebration of the vitality of the bank and the region. These stories highlight the contributions of hundreds of individuals in our area. They are stories of innovative thinking and great partnering. They acknowledge the value of education and of giving back. They demonstrate the power and heart of community.

These are the stories that I heard as a child and experienced as an adult. Reading them, you will understand how I have been inspired by those who went before me and those I have worked beside. You'll see why I am confident that our area's young leaders, with their own passions and own partnerships, will continue to build and strengthen our community, and our future.

The 150-year history of Baker Boyer Bank is integral to the history of Walla Walla, the region, and the people who have lived here and do live here today. It's a history of a community that has come about and continues to grow because of partnerships, trust, and innovation. It is rare for a family business to continue for 150 years. We are fortunate to have a strong foundation laid by our founder D.S. Baker. We know Baker Boyer is only as strong as the families, businesses, land, and culture around us and we have never forgotten that our success is born only *after* the communities we serve succeed. Our mission is to partner with local families to help them build and secure their own legacies.

I have had the privilege to lead Baker Boyer and help steward the company to this milestone anniversary. Through the succession of six generations of the Baker family, from our founding to today, we have followed a principle my great-great grandfather practiced: What is good for the long-term health of the community is good for the long-term health of the bank. To this day, Baker Boyer has been driven by this core belief. It is our family legacy.

Deep down I have strong sentimental feelings for my hometown. This way of doing business, what we call "The Walla Walla Way," continues to thrive, making the area a gem and a wonderful place to live. It is a town I left in my early 20's convinced there was a better place. I wised up when we started our family and made the best decision of our lives—we moved back to a community that is a superstar among towns. I am proud to call myself a Walla Wallan.

I know you will recognize hope in The Walla Walla Way spread across the pages ahead. These stories about the bank, its clients, and the community honor what has been, celebrate what is now, and give promise to what will be. I believe they will inspire you, as they have inspired us, to do great things and give back to your own community.

These are the stories that I heard as a child and experienced as an adult. Reading them, you will understand how I have been inspired by those who went before me and those I have worked beside. You'll see why I am confident that our area's young leaders, with their own passions and own partnerships, will continue to build and strengthen our community, and our future.

— Megan Clubb

Baker-Boyer Bank Building
Walla Walla, Washington.

Baker Boyer Bank founder Dorsey S. Baker appears in the inset of this panoramic illustration of Walla Walla drawn in 1884 by Lucien R. Burleigh.

CHAPTER 1

150 Years a Pioneer

"I find the evidence of an extraordinary willpower, rare business sagacity and a farsightedness which inspired him to persevere and triumph where more timid men held back and took refuge in the commonplace."

— *Whitman College President Stephen Penrose*

Not too long ago, Walla Walla locals could proudly say their town, three to six hours from major Pacific Northwest cities and 40-some miles from the nearest interstate highway, was "the best kept secret" in Washington State.

After all, they enjoyed three colleges—along with the arts and culture they share with the community—as well as the oldest continuously operating symphony west of the Mississippi River, safe streets, congenial neighborhoods where the wealthy and working class lived side by side, well-supported public schools, a moderate four-seasons climate, and plentiful outdoor recreation. All at an affordable cost of living.

Then came the internet and its global reach, through which national publications and tourism and lifestyle bloggers began posting "Top-10" and "Best of" lists in myriad categories. But before Walla Walla—a town previously noted mostly for its state penitentiary and its famous sweet onions, the official state vegetable—began hitting the charts, two factors coalesced to launch it onto the world scene.

The annual Wheelin' Walla Walla Weekend is a big draw for fans of classic automobiles.

First was an effort by local businesses in the late 1990s to restore downtown Main Street buildings to their brick-and-masonry Victorian and Beaux-Arts glory of a century before. It paid off, with Walla Walla in 2001 winning the National Trust for Historic Preservation's Great American Main Street Award.

The second factor was wine. By the 1980s the world at large could no longer ignore the fact that Washington State, with its microclimates and diverse soils, could produce European varietals every bit as good as—and often better than—California and French wines. Walla Walla had one commercial winery in 1977: Leonetti Cellar. Two more quickly followed: Woodward Canyon in 1981 and L'Ecole N° 41 in 1983. Those initial three established a far-reaching reputation for superior quality that attracted other vintners—several from Europe—to the Walla Walla Valley appellation. The growing region, which also includes part of northern Umatilla County in Oregon, now boasts more than 120 premium wineries.

On the vintners' heels, the new wine culture sparked a boom of gourmet restaurateurs from major cities and an influx of downtown tasting rooms that offered expanded venues for artists and musicians. With the ensuing flood of well-heeled wine tourists,

Washington's "best kept secret" was secret no more. The city's website today lists 65 national and regional awards Walla Walla has received since 2000. Among them are "best" awards as a place to visit, to live, to retire, for businesses and careers, as a global wine region, as a food town, as a "most beautiful town," and twice as the "friendliest town" in America.

In addition, Walla Walla's Whitman College is perennially ranked among the nation's top private liberal arts schools. And in 2013, Walla Walla Community College was the winner of the Aspen Institute's prize as the best two-year school in the nation, largely due to its partnerships with agriculture, wine, culinary arts, wind energy, environmental conservation, and other regional industries in creating programs to train workers.

Fortunately for the city, ever since the first trickle of westward immigrants to the Pacific Northwest in the late 1840s, the Walla Walla Valley has proved fertile ground for bold-thinking people to build a thriving community.

Walla Walla's warm summers, moderate winters, and access to irrigation have made agriculture the mainstay of its economy since the beginning. Local commerce received a boost in the late 1850s when a chance at Idaho gold brought a flood of prospectors to Walla Walla to spend the winter and purchase supplies before returning to their claims. But when the placer mining played out in a few years, agriculture—wheat and cattle in particular—remained and expanded as the town grew from settlement to city. In 1856 it officially was chartered as a city and the seat of the Washington territorial Walla Walla County. Until Washington was granted statehood in 1889, Walla Walla County included lands east of the Cascade Mountains, across northern Idaho, and into Western Montana.

By 1870, Walla Walla's first census stood at 1,394 souls—more populous than the small lumber and port town of Seattle and the yet-to-be-established city of Spokane. But those two cities would see major economic and population growth with completion of the national east-west Great Northern Railroad in the 1890s, which bypassed Walla Walla. By the end of that decade, however, the city, with a population of about 10,000, had a nucleus of economic diversity, government, schools, and churches that would help the community overcome setbacks that would cripple, if not wipe out, lesser small towns.

Through all the years, from immigrant settlement to the city it is today, businesses have come and gone. But one has endured and thrived: Baker Boyer National Bank. Chartered in 1869, Baker Boyer is celebrating its 150th anniversary. It began as a mercantile 10 years earlier to supply local farmers and a rush of prospectors heading to and from newly discovered gold fields in Idaho. When the miners returned to winter in Walla Walla, they entrusted their leather pouches of gold dust and nuggets to a safe in the mercantile and its owner, Dorsey "Doc" Syng Baker.

Baker's legacy is inextricably linked to the development of the city and region, with his "genius" for enterprise, community development, and philanthropy alive today among descendants. His own personal story is a triumphant tale in the building of the Pacific Northwest, although one with austere beginnings.

A "Pauper" on the Plains

Dorsey Baker stood heartbroken and humiliated that day on the open prairie in the summer of 1848, when a growing love affair came to an abrupt end.

Northstar Winery hosts a harvest dinner for food and wine aficionados.

Diners enjoy a meal on the patio near the hand-wound clock that has been keeping time for Main Street passers-by since 1906.

An adventurer, the son of Puritan parentage who was born on October 13, 1823, Dorsey had left Illinois in the spring of '48 and joined a wagon train heading for the West on the Oregon Trail. He was lured, like countless thousands who made the hard, perilous journey across primeval plains and mountains, by tales of rich lands and opportunities on the far side of the American continent for those with grit and gumption. His father, Ezra Baker, had carved out such a life for his family in Wabash County, Illinois, as a doctor, farmer, flour mill operator, and merchant. Dorsey wanted to create the same for himself, but wouldn't be content with being just a settler. His nature was more visionary.

But first came that matter of the heart that shook his confidence more than a thousand miles and several months into his journey to the sparsely populated settlement of Portland, Oregon.

Dorsey had signed on to the wagon train three years after graduating from the Jefferson Medical College in Philadelphia, Pennsylvania. With few possessions other than a medical bag and a horse and buggy to carry him, rather than an ox-drawn covered wagon, he agreed to provide physician services on the trek in exchange for food and supplies. Along the way he met a young woman, the daughter of another member of the wagon train, and they quickly grew fond of each other.

"Her father objected to this, giving as a reason that he did not purpose to have his daughter marry a pauper," Dorsey's son, W.W. "Will" Baker, wrote in a 1934 biography of his father titled *Forty Years a Pioneer*. "Dr. Baker said that while he, himself, knew that he was

Dorsey Syng Baker as a young man.

Walla Walla's Main Street in 1886 was a center for business and socializing. The group of buildings on the right were known as "Union Block." On the left are the Reynolds-Day Building, the Paine Building, the Seil Building, and Baker Boyer Bank.

The first immigrant wagon train arrives in the Walla Walla Valley in this 1842 illustration.

extremely poor, he was not aware that this fact had become general knowledge, and thereupon resolved to extricate himself from the pauper class at the earliest opportunity." But building wealth for himself was not his sole objective; the doctor wanted to use it to carve out a healthy community in the raw West, complete with commerce, education, and sound, practical leaders to ensure it would endure.

Mortified as he was at the father's rejection, Dorsey was not one to dwell on anger and hurt feelings, especially his own. It was an attitude instilled in him by his mother, Elizabeth Haupt Baker, whom Dorsey deeply loved and respected for her wisdom and strength of character. She'd written a letter to her son five years earlier, in 1843, before he left home to supervise the shipment of produce via flatboats down the Mississippi River to New Orleans. The oldest known document authored by a member of the Baker family, it sheds light on her beliefs and advises her son as he heads into the world his own man.

"Through faith, love and humility you will be enabled to govern yourself, though it will be a difficult task and will require constant self-observation to see and subdue the rising passions . . . ," his mother wrote. "Human nature is prone to evil. That moment you are tempted, lift your heart to God and you will feel comfort. . . . The best way to overcome Anger is

to be silent and never even use expressions of the countenance, for they are as mean as angry words. 'Be angry and sin not. Let not the sun go down upon thy wrath.' " The letter also cautioned him against drinking, smoking, gambling, and partaking in other vices, as well as providing advice to "promote health, respect and cleanliness."

"I have imparted my whole soul to you because you are dear to me," the letter concluded. "And if you should be cast away among strangers in a strange land, God will care for you if you will obey these precepts. . . . As this may be the last letter I shall ever write to you, keep it as a passport; carry it with you where you cannot lose it."

Dorsey had the letter with him that day on the Oregon Trail when he was labeled a pauper. He is said by his family to have kept the letter close at hand until his death 40 years later, on July 5, 1888. In those intervening years—by his wit, business acumen, determination, hands, and back—he became rich in wealth, family, friends, and reputation as a pioneering figure in the development of the Inland Northwest. His enterprises ranged from farming to cattle ranching, railroad building to lumbering, from starting general stores to, ultimately, founding a bank in Walla Walla with his brother-in-law, John Franklin Boyer.

Dorsey Baker's son W.W. Baker (left), author of Forty Years a Pioneer, stands with his cousin, a son of John F. Boyer, in front of Baker Boyer Bank, circa 1880s.

Portrait of a Pioneer

No personal diary survives that could provide a glimpse into the thoughts, guiding philosophies, and beliefs that Dorsey Baker lived by. "He was a person who rarely wasted words," W.W. Baker recalled. But enough has been written about him by his descendants, scholars, and others to get a sense of his vision and genius in business and building. He also was frugal, task oriented, and intensely self-driven, and he formed strong partnerships to start and grow his diverse enterprises.

Forty Years a Pioneer, in which W.W. Baker, born in 1861, focused almost entirely on his father's business exploits, with little reference to his home life, is largely based on experiences his father imparted to him, recorded transactions, letters, and information from other reliable sources. The younger Baker was the last of seven children born during his father's first marriage, which ended after 13 years with the death of his wife, Caroline Tibbetts Baker, in 1863, at age 29. Three of those seven children died in infancy. Dorsey Baker would have two more marriages, one short-lived with the death of Mary Legier soon after their wedding in 1865, and lastly, in 1867, to Elizabeth Millican Horton McCullough. Their marriage through the rest of Dorsey Baker's life produced eight children, four of whom died in childhood during a diphtheria epidemic.

"He was a stern man—harsh often," W.W. Baker, who served as the bank's fourth president, wrote of his father, "but these were harsh times when men fought for their existence, and with bare hands wrested their living from the very earth itself."

Dorsey had a softer side, too. W.W. Baker also recalled his father at home and in the evening by the firelight "studying his Bible or reading selected authors, for he was a student—kindly and genial, and always generous to his friends and neighbors."

The son also took note of a short poem his father wrote, found in his business records:

Honor and truth were given to cherish;
Cherish them then, though all else
should take flight;
Landmarks are these which never should perish,
Stars that will shine in the darkest night.

Another biography of Dorsey Baker, *Gold, Rawhide and Iron*, written by Helen Baker Reynolds, offers impressions of her grandfather, who died eight years before she was born in 1896. The daughter of Dorsey's eldest child, Edwin Franklin, and Sarah Ann (Miller) Baker, she recalled that in her parents' stories of the pioneer days, "Grandfather loomed always as a central figure—a dominant and all but incredible figure, rather like a lesser Paul Bunyan."

She grew up in a home where two portraits of her grandfather were prominently displayed. One was a photograph taken when he was a young man, perhaps during his first marriage.

Dorsey Baker family home in Walla Walla.

Dorsey Baker in his prime as a banker, entrepreneur, and community builder.

Baker a few years before his death in 1888.

What Reynolds described in the photo was "a strong young face, clean-shaven except for a line of short beard marking the angular jaw—an intensely serious face, thoughtful and rather gloomy. The brooding expression in the deep-set eyes once caused a visitor in our home to ask, 'Is that man a poet?' . . . Yet the eyes of the man in the picture are indeed the eyes of one who saw visions. And perhaps, if his talents had taken a slightly different turn, Dorsey Baker might have been creative in the realm of the arts. As it was, those eyes, so intense and direct . . . were seeking forms of creation of a strictly practical sort."

In the second portrait, a painting of her white-haired grandfather in his final years, Reynolds saw "a man grown hoary, tremendously bearded and austere, with facial lines still strong" and still with that penetrating gaze. "Vaguely, I identified it with the Almighty in His more implacable moods," she wrote.

Yet Dorsey Baker's life from the time he left Illinois for a new life out West was not without its Jobian struggles. The deaths of two wives and seven of the 15 children he fathered cannot have been easily endured. No doubt it was a mountain of grief one can never fully recover from, but Dorsey clearly persevered, continuing to build his family's legacy.

His own health was precarious as well. The Baker patriarch had twice suffered strokes that partially paralyzed his left side, and were the source of frequent pain and muscular weakness. It's not clear in family records when the strokes occurred, but the first is said to have happened sometime in his youth. The second came during a return trip from Oregon to Illinois via the Isthmus of Panama to visit his parents in 1857, just a few years before he came to Walla Walla to start a mercantile.

His mental and physical hardships, however, did not keep him from undertaking his many pursuits. Rather, Reynolds wrote, her grandfather's sense that his life might be short lent an urgency to take on and overcome hardships of travel and community building in what was still mostly wilderness. He would stand little "tomfoolishness," she wrote, neither in his businesses, partners, and politicians, nor in others with whom he associated—and certainly not in himself.

"When I try to discover the factors which contributed to his outstanding influence in the community," Whitman College President Stephen B.L. Penrose wrote in 1934 for inclusion into W.W. Baker's book, "I find the evidence of an extraordinary willpower, rare business sagacity and a farsightedness which inspired him to persevere and triumph where more timid men held back and took refuge in the commonplace. Perhaps your father did not have that sort of leadership which inspires other men to join wholeheartedly in a common undertaking because he was too bold and self-reliant to feel the need for other men to make his enterprises a success. I suppose there is always a quality of impatience in a truly strong man who feels himself held back by other men's timidity or weakness."

CONFLICT AND CHANGE IN THE NORTHWEST

Much history had occurred during non-native settlement of the Pacific Northwest before Dorsey Baker arrived in Portland on the wagon train in September 1848. Still more would occur—much of it involving bloody clashes over lands amongst indigenous tribes, waves of settlers, and miners, with soldiers sent to try to keep the peace and protect the latter two—before Baker made his way to Walla Walla 11 years later.

On August 14, 1848, when Baker was still on the trail west with his wagon train, President James Polk had authorized the incorporation of the Oregon Territory. The vast tract included what are now the states of Oregon, Washington, and Idaho, plus the western sectors of Montana and Wyoming up to the Continental Divide in the Rocky Mountains. In 1853 the region was split to create the Washington Territory, which included northern Idaho, northwestern Montana, and what would become Washington State in 1889.

The home of many Native American tribes for thousands of years, the region's first known non-indigenous exploration of the land was conducted by Meriwether Lewis and William Clark from 1804 to 1806. Their Corps of Discovery blazed a trail that began near St. Louis and generally followed the Missouri River to its headwaters, then scaled the Rockies before heading down to the Pacific Ocean via the Snake and Columbia Rivers. The Corps' objectives were to search for an inland waterway to the Pacific from the Mississippi River, map the region, note its fauna and flora, and make contacts with the indigenous tribes.

They found no navigable waterway that would provide a route from the Atlantic to the Pacific Coast without having to voyage around the tip of South America. But what they did observe and record in their journals attracted commerce, first in the fur trade. Then came other trailblazers, such as Jedediah Smith and others, who marked fur-trapping routes in the West that also provided directions for "the

A band of the Cayuse tribe lived in the Walla Walla Valley until after the signing of the Treaty of 1855 with the U.S. government. The Cayuse, and other tribes in the Pacific Northwest, were then resettled on reservations. Top: Children of local tribe member Mo-Ta-Nic. Bottom: Pe-Tow-Wa (lower left) was over 100 years old at the time of this photo.

U.S. Army soldiers, Second Cavalry, Troop G, muster at Fort Walla Walla in 1886.

missionary, the gold-seeker and land-hungry emigrant," wrote Whitman College political science professor Chester C. Maxey in 1953, when he was president of the college. By the 1840s, the skirmishes and wars with the indigenous tribes over land and culture had begun and would not come to an end for 40 years, with the tribes stripped of their ways and relegated to reservations.

Those wars began with a pivotal moment in the Walla Walla Valley, known as the Whitman Incident, and led to the establishment of a U.S. Army fort around which a settlement would grow to become the city of Walla Walla. In 1836, Dr. Marcus Whitman and his wife, Narcissa, established a Protestant mission in the valley to offer religious instruction and health services to local tribes. But as settlers began arriving, the mission grew to be known as a wayside where immigrants heading for Oregon could replenish provisions and find treatment for illnesses and injuries. A measles outbreak grew into a deadly epidemic for indigenous tribes who had no previous exposure to it.

"The more Dr. Whitman did to treat the sick, the more the conviction spread that he was killing them with some subtle poison," Maxey wrote in a history of the valley. "Indians now came to fear them as malevolent sorcerers, and Dr. Whitman most of all. There could be no safety for the red man, it seemed apparent, until the evil hexers were exterminated."

In Cayuse culture, traditionally if a medicine man's patient died in his care, relatives had the right to seek revenge. From a Cayuse perspective, the measles was an Anglo-American disease that the Whitmans, who practiced medicine and were therefore Anglo-American healers, should know how to cure. A belief grew that the Whitmans were killing the Cayuse people through an application of evil spells and there was a need to protect the people by killing the practitioners.

On November 29, 1847, a band of Cayuse attacked the mission, killing Whitman, his wife, and 12 others. Word of the attack spread throughout the region and touched off the first of many battles with indigenous tribes in the territory over the next 30 years. In June of 1855, a council held in the Walla Walla Valley produced a treaty that established the Yakama, Nez Perce, and Confederated Tribes of the Umatilla reservations, with the ceding of all remaining tribal lands to the United States. But the boundaries meant little to arriving immigrants, and the next year the Army established Fort Walla Walla along the banks of Mill Creek. From there the cavalry were sent to fight tribes resisting settlement in northeastern Washington Territory, with the Nez Perce wars concluding in 1877.

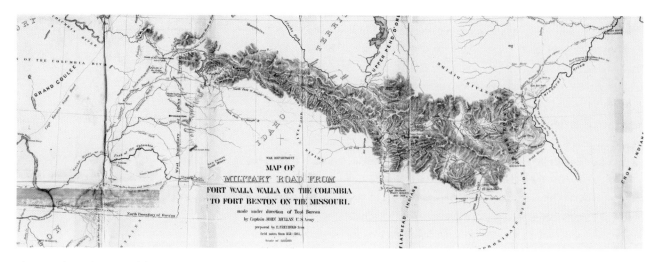

This map shows the route of the 625-mile Mullan Road from Fort Walla Walla across the Rockies to Fort Benton in Montana.

The fort also served another purpose. It would be the nucleus around which the small Walla Walla settlement surrounding it would grow into the inland Pacific Northwest's hub of commerce for farmers and miners, and the businesses that catered to their needs. For a few years the city would be the largest west of Minneapolis and north of San Francisco.

WALLA WALLA BOUND

The valley was relatively easy to access from the Pacific via the Columbia and Walla Walla Rivers, and from the south using a spur of the Oregon Trail. But only a patchwork of trails served travel to and from the north and east. That was rectified in 1860 when Lt. John Mullan and a crew of soldiers and civilians completed the initial 625-mile road from Fort Walla Walla across the Rockies to Fort Benton on the plains of Montana, where the upper Missouri River was still a navigable waterway to the Mississippi. As it happened, the year the so-called Mullan Road was finished a gold rush began in Idaho that drew tens of thousands of treasure seekers to the region, many of whom would depend on Walla Walla for supplies.

Although Dorsey Baker was penniless when he arrived in Portland in 1848, his personal toolbox for building a new life in the West was his knowledge as a physician and what he had learned as the son of an Illinois farmer and merchant. He began in Portland as a doctor to its several hundred residents, but in 1849 he was lured to the booming gold fields of California. It would be a short but successful stay, and in January 1850 he returned to Portland with merchandise worth a total of $1,800 to begin a mercantile. He founded D.S. Baker and Company with a partner. It sold groceries, hardware, farm implements, guns, footwear, and other general merchandise, much of it purchased in San Francisco and shipped by sea to Portland.

That June he married Caroline Tibbetts, and over the next nine years he would travel the trails of Oregon and northern California on business and personal scouting trips. During that time he also built a flour mill, and began a cattle business.

But his sights remained over the horizon. And with gold being discovered in Idaho, and the Mullan Road under construction to create a more direct northern land route to Walla Walla from the Midwest, he sold his shares in the mercantile in the spring of 1859 and started a new one in the booming young town of Walla Walla that fall.

On June 30, 1860, Baker wrote a statement of his personal worth, starting with zero at the time he arrived in Oregon nearly a dozen years before. W.W. Baker included the list of resources and liabilities in his book. On the resources side were accounts and bills receivable, currency, the Walla Walla mercantile, cattle, wagons and ox teams, real estate in Portland and Umpqua, and one safe, among a few other assets. The total value came to $43,014 and change. Today that amount is equivalent to about $1.3 million. He listed no outstanding liabilities.

Once rejected as a pauper, Baker would continue to grow, as he created a new role for himself in Walla Walla: Dorsey S. Baker, Banker. And the family he moved from Portland in 1861 would also grow, with more children and successive generations integrating themselves into the social and economic fabric of Walla Walla to take part in its continuing evolution.

Dorsey Baker sold his first-floor mercantile on Second Avenue to Paine Brothers & Moore in 1869. He moved his banking operation to the upper floor of the building, with a sign on top of the façade simply calling it "Bank Place," circa 1870.

A Vision Realized

In Walla Walla, everywhere you look today, Baker's influence is evident. The seven-story steel-frame Baker Boyer National Bank building itself, built in 1911 and briefly the tallest in the state, sits on the same corner of Second Avenue and Main Street that his mercantile once occupied.

East of downtown is Whitman College, where generations of Baker descendants have been educated. When it began as a seminary founded by Congregational Church Rev. Cushing Eells in 1866, Baker donated the original four acres on which it was built.

Baker's commitment to education didn't end there. He also donated land a few blocks north of the bank in 1866 to build the first public school in Washington Territory east of the Cascades. It was later named Baker School in his honor after he donated money to expand it. Further demonstrating its commitment to education, the bank in 1882 donated $1,000 to help build Walla Walla College on land that would grow into the city of College Place, adjacent to Walla Walla's western city limits. That amount today would be the equivalent of more than $26,270.

A few blocks from the bank is the *Walla Walla Union-Bulletin*, initially founded in 1869 as the *Walla Walla Union*. Believing the town should have a newspaper to compete with the existing *Washington Statesman* to give readers a diversity of editorial and political views, Baker bought the presses and had them shipped from San Francisco for a total of $2,437.

Extending in all directions and over the horizon into the Palouse region are wheat fields, some initially fenced and planted by Baker in the early 1860s, when he demonstrated to bottomland farmers that the vast hill country could be used for more than just livestock grazing.

To the west runs a railroad bed he constructed and financed mostly out of his

The seven-story, iron-frame Baker Boyer Bank Building was, for a short time, the tallest building west of the Mississippi when completed in 1911.

Baker-Boyer Bank Building. Walla Walla, Wash.

own pocket in the 1870s to move wheat 31 miles to the Columbia River port of Wallula for shipment by steamboat to Portland and world markets. Previously, wheat grown in the area was delivered by wagon. The short line, narrow-gauge railroad to Walla Walla would prove far more economical for growers, and that spurred major growth in wheat acreage.

Several miles south is Umatilla County, Oregon, where, in the forests of the Blue Mountains, Baker undertook his last enterprise. In the 1880s he built a sawmill and flume there to bring lumber and wood fuel to a railroad branch line for transport to the rapidly growing city of Walla Walla.

Dorsey Baker's final resting place is on the south edge of Walla Walla at Mountain View Cemetery. Surrounding a black granite monument inscribed with the family name, 71 rectangular blocks of granite in a circular family plot mark the passing of Baker and his wives, children, and descendants through the years. Established by the city in 1853, the cemetery grounds were barren until Baker planted a few trees and shrubs, and personally hauled water to nurture them. He later bequeathed the funds for the cemetery's original watering system, acknowledged by a fountain erected in 1902 in his memory.

For an article marking the state's first centennial in 1989, longtime *Union-Bulletin* reporter and columnist Vance Orchard asked retired state librarian Nancy Pryor, who was transcribing Dorsey Baker's papers for inclusion into Whitman College's archives, what she believed were the strengths of Baker's contributions.

"Obviously the building of the railroad and the bank were big things, but my feeling is because he was an educated man, he probably did more than any single person to improve the quality of life in Walla Walla" through his commitment to its colleges and schools, Pryor responded. "His contributions added much to elevating cultural aspects of the young [Whitman] college and the equally young town. I think Dr. Baker set the tone of the times in Walla Walla. This town has always had a bit more intellectual stature, a bit nicer living and cultural level than many cities of 25,000 in the U.S. and much of the credit for that goes to Dr. Baker and of course, people like him, too."

Walla Walla Bulletin *employees gather for a company photo circa 1908. The Bulletin competed with the Walla Walla Union, founded in 1869 with the help of Dorsey Baker. Baker bought and donated the Union's first printing press. The two papers merged in 1934 as the* Walla Walla Union-Bulletin.

Mountain View Cemetery in Walla Walla is the site of Baker Circle, where 71 rectangular granite stones mark the graves of Dorsey Baker and generations of his extended family.

JOHN F. BOYER

DORSEY SYNG BAKER and John Franklin Boyer were like yin and yang partners at the bank they founded in 1869, each bringing separate strengths that, combined, proved a complementary formula for success.

While Baker was the entrepreneurial visionary, always seeking new enterprises to develop, Boyer was the partner who ran the day-to-day operations at Baker Boyer Bank. And while Baker had a reputation for being on the taciturn side of communications, Boyer was a people person.

"He was a lovable and sociable man, always warm hearted and charitable," noted a bank publication to commemorate its 50th anniversary in 1919. "He never denied the needy or forsook the unfortunate."

John F. Boyer.

Baker and Boyer also had much in common—not the least of which was that they were brothers-in-law after Boyer married Baker's sister, Sarah Elizabeth, in 1853. Both men had crossed the plains as young men seeking to build their future, Baker to Portland in 1848 and Boyer to California in 1849. Out West, both had opened mercantiles in gold mining districts and maintained reputations as honest men who cared about their customers and the communities in which they lived. And both were financial contributors in the establishment of Whitman Seminary and the college it would grow into, sharing a belief that settling and building the West depended on having an educated citizenry.

Historian Frank T. Gilbert, who profiled Boyer's life in 1882, described his success not as chance or favorable turn of fortune's wheel but achieved "by the exercise of economy, industry and business integrity, guided with intelligent financial ability."

Boyer was born on March 28, 1824, in Rockcastle County, Kentucky, moving in infancy with his family to the Ohio River and later to Jefferson County, Indiana. At the age of 25, in 1849, he joined the throngs hoping to strike it rich in the California gold fields.

He had some success with mining but discovered that more opportunity lay in outfitting and supplying miners, so he parlayed his earnings into opening a mercantile in the gold-rush town of Sonora. Hard luck hit in 1852, however, when the store was ravaged by fire, destroying most of Boyer's property.

He married Sarah Baker in Illinois and they remained in the East until 1859, when the couple headed to California via ship and overland through the Isthmus of Panama to San Francisco and on to Sonora. There, Boyer reestablished himself as a merchant until 1862, when he accepted his brother-in-law's offer of a partnership in Dorsey Baker's mercantile in the then-gold-rush town of Walla Walla. Boyer, without having to invest money in the business, received a third of its profits under the arrangement.

Much of the operation of the store—including its nascent banking practices—was left to Boyer as Baker tended to other enterprises. When the gold fields played out, taking away the miners, the partners decided to sell their store and go all-in on developing the bank.

Gilbert described the bank in 1882 as "one of the most reliable monied institutions on the Pacific Coast. Not because of the extensive funds invested, that only reaches $150,000 . . . but because the bank risks no money upon uncertain outside speculations."

After Dorsey S. Baker died in 1888 and the bank received a federal charter as Baker Boyer National Bank in 1889, John F. Boyer was elected its first president—a title he retained until his own death in 1897, a month before his 73rd birthday. He also held many other titles, each noting his commitment to community building and education. He was elected Walla Walla County treasurer for six consecutive two-year terms. For 30 years he was a board of trustees member and treasurer of Whitman Seminary and College, elected to board chairman a few months before he died. He also served as vestryman and warden of St. Paul's Episcopal Church.

"It was a motto of his from early youth that a man is the architect of his own future," the bank's 50th-anniversary publication said of Boyer, "so he strove manfully to make the structure of his character worthy of all honorable mention. As a result, every success ever won to him . . . was due to industry, politeness, native wit and honorable means."

Acting honorably was also something Boyer and Baker had in common, and something they instilled in their children, according to Gilbert. "Each and every one of those children has been educated to look upon life, not as the idle drones upon the honey stored for them by the working bees in the hive, but as a period blocked out of time, in which they are to accomplish something by their own acts that will not be discreditable to themselves and the name they bear," he wrote. "To Dr. Baker, to J.F. Boyer, and men of their kind, Eastern Washington Territory owes its present prosperity and future prospects."

John F. Boyer wrote this 1891 letter marked "confidential" to the Rev. Myron Eells of the Congregational Church during a period of financial hardship for the college. A Whitman trustee and treasurer for 30 years, Boyer expressed his and others' concerns about "our Presbyterian friends' willingness to take the college off our hands." Ultimately, Whitman remained in the Congregational Church until it became nondenominational in 1907.

This two-story brick building housed the Baker & Boyer mercantile in 1861. The mercantile also offered basic banking services and safe-keeping for miners' pouches of gold. It was sold to Paine Brothers & Moore in 1869 and Baker Boyer Bank was established on the upper floor.

CHAPTER 2

Playing for Keeps

It wasn't much to look at, the rough-hewn, 20-by-40-foot log building that in 1859 served as the mercantile Dorsey S. Baker established on Second Avenue in Walla Walla. It was, however, a catalyst for commerce in eastern Washington Territory.

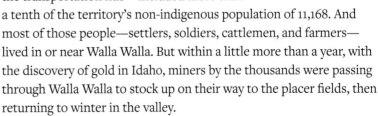

Rudimentary sketch of Dorsey Baker's first mercantile store in 1859.

Walla Walla County's sprawling boundaries in those days—with Walla Walla the transportation hub—included more than a tenth of the territory's non-indigenous population of 11,168. And most of those people—settlers, soldiers, cattlemen, and farmers— lived in or near Walla Walla. But within a little more than a year, with the discovery of gold in Idaho, miners by the thousands were passing through Walla Walla to stock up on their way to the placer fields, then returning to winter in the valley.

The first shipment of merchandise Baker ordered was shipped to the store from Portland on October 7, 1859, at a cost of $25,101. It consisted of dry goods, boots and shoes, groceries, hardware, and firearms. The delivery also included one thing no one else had in the region—a large safe. As was typical for gold rush towns, Walla Walla was also growing in the number of saloons and bordellos, as well as bandits and other unsavory types who would gladly relieve miners of their diggings. But the safe, under the watch of Baker and the day-to-day operations manager he hired, William Stephens, proved an oasis of trust, if not comfort, for miners. It would also mark the beginnings of Baker's banking career, as he received deposits, bought gold to trade in San Francisco for a profit, and made loans.

Baker Boyer Bank built its second building in 1890 on the same block where its original bank stood. The bank soon outgrew this building as well, and it was razed for its current seven-story building completed in 1911.

His reputation for dealing fairly and honestly with customers was not lost on miners, who in increasing numbers left their pouches of gold dust with him for safekeeping. Indeed, so much gold was left with Baker that the safe was full and nail kegs were used to manage the overflow. In exchange for holding the gold, depositors were charged $5 a month.

"Not even a solitary sentinel guarded this treasure by day or night," W.W. Baker, a boy at the time, wrote about his recollections of how the system worked. "To each bag of gold dust, the name of the owner was securely attached, and then it was thrown into a common pile. No receipts were given and no questions were asked. Losses never occurred, and there were no controversies that arose covering these transactions involving hundreds of thousands of dollars of gold dust."

This is believed to be Baker Boyer Bank's original safe, brought by Dorsey Baker to Walla Walla in 1859 and used to store gold pouches for miners.

"Do No Harm"

In a sense, Baker, the merchant and banker, was practicing the oath he took when he became a doctor in 1845. Physicians then, as now, vowed to do no harm and earn the confidence of patients by providing each a full measure of service and devotion. The economic health of the mercantile, and in turn its customers and the overall community, Baker knew, depended on it. It was a guiding philosophy he and partner John F. Boyer kept uppermost in mind when they sold the mercantile in 1869 and officially formed Baker Boyer Bank. (It would be nationally chartered in 1888.) The culture has also been passed down to the nine bank presidents succeeding them.

Megan Clubb, great-great-granddaughter of Dorsey Baker and the bank's chair of the board in 2019, learned "do no harm" as the daughter of Baker Ferguson, who presided over the bank from 1965 to 1982 and had learned it from his Baker forebears.

"I would say the key has been that there's this sense that family is number one. And by that I mean not as a factor to overall nurturing each other to the benefit of us, but the value of time spent with family—men and women passing along stories, passing along their values to the next generation," said Clubb, who was the bank's president and CEO from 2000 to 2014 and also served as a director with the Federal Reserve Bank of San Francisco.

"I've told many people I was born with a silver spoon in my mouth. There weren't very many people that were born with more advantages than I had," she said. "There was never a doubt in my mind as a kid, when my dad was talking to me or my grandfather was talking to me, it was understood that 'You're privileged. You better do something with it . . . You need to help others.' "

In one conversation with her father when she was 10, she recalled him telling her that essentially what the bank does is "rent money. And

A sign-carrying young Megan Clubb fronts a band to herald the opening of First National Bank of Oregon branch in Beaverton in 1960. She was there with her father, Baker Ferguson, the Oregon bank's director of marketing at that time.

that sounds potentially off-putting," she said. "But his point was that we need to have what we give people returned to us. If they are put into a position where they can't return to us what we've given them, we are not serving them. It's bad for them, and it's bad for us. In 2008, after the subprime lending crisis, I saw exactly what Dad was saying as the world watched nearly 10 million families across the United States lose their homes.

"Debt is such a strange and unique product," Clubb said. "There are very few products that you have to be careful whom you give it to and how much you give." It was a core value that had carried the bank from its early days and through the Great Depression in the 1930s. And it would serve Clubb in her decision-making that saw the bank emerge from the nation's 2008 financial collapse unscathed and in a stronger position.

NAVIGATING THE DEPRESSION

During the Depression more than 9,000 banks failed, with some 4,000 going out of business in 1933 alone. And because deposits were uninsured at the time, as banks failed, people lost their savings. By 1933 an estimated $140 billion in deposits—the equivalent of about $2.7 trillion in today's dollars—had simply vanished.

Economists still argue various theories on the root causes of the financial collapse, ranging from a highly leveraged and speculative stock market, to adherence to the gold standard, to a too-tightly controlled money supply, among other factors. And which of those underlying dominoes fell first? But the cascade of calamity in the 1930s began with the stock market crash in 1929, followed by personal and business bankruptcies, and failures of overextended

CONSTRUCTION OF THE 1911 BUILDING

banks—all leading to massive poverty and a national unemployment rate of about 25 percent by 1933.

On February 14 of that year, however, W.W. Baker read a reaffirming message that the family bank he had been presiding over since 1919 was a beacon of light amid the current bleakness. The message was in the form of a proclamation from Walla Walla Mayor Frank H. Richmond. Using his authority to "act for the common good, peace, happiness and financial welfare of our citizens," the mayor had proclaimed a two-month bank closure to protect depositors with two local institutions: First National Bank of Walla Walla and the Union Bank and Trust Company of Walla Walla. The time was needed so they could "reform their financial program."

Baker Boyer National Bank, however, was allowed to remain open due to its sound financial health and practices. Along with Richmond's proclamation, the *Walla Walla Daily Bulletin* published an accompanying editorial: "It should not be necessary to remind the people of Walla Walla that there continues open and in operation here one bank, the oldest in the state, an institution recognized as one of the strongest financial concerns in the West," it stated. "Financial statements of the bank, as published at regular intervals, have always shown an excellent condition and the same principles and ideals which saw this institution through the early pioneer days continue to prevail."

A month after Richmond's proclamation, President Franklin D. Roosevelt declared a nationwide four-day closure so that Department of the Treasury reviewers could examine each bank to determine its soundness. Unfortunately for smaller, more remote banks like Baker Boyer, the closure lasted quite a bit longer than just four days while they waited for the bank examiners, and customers could not withdraw any of their deposits. But

Bank Holiday
Is Proclaimed
For 2 In City

PROCLAMATION

WHEREAS, on account of the financial conditions surrounding the First National Bank of Walla Walla and the Union Bank and Trust Company of Walla Walla, it is deemed advisable in order to protect their depositors that a period of time be granted in which to reform their financial program.

NOW THEREFORE I, Frank H. Richmond, as mayor of the City of Walla Walla, by virtue of the authority in me vested to act for the common good, peace, happiness and financial welfare of our citizens, do hereby declare and appoint the days beginning February 14, and ending April 15, 1933, and all intervening days, holidays in the city of Walla Walla, Washington, for said First National Bank and Union Bank and Trust Company.

FRANK H. RICHMOND
Mayor of the City of
Walla Walla. Wash.

Under this appeared editorial:

It should not be necessary to remind the people of Walla Walla that there continues open and in operation here one bank, the oldest in the state, an institution recognized as one of the strongest financial concerns in the West.

With such a bank in the community tere is indeed reason for confidence and a high degree of reassurance that business will go on.

Financial statement of the bank as published at regular intervals have always shown an escellent condition and the same principals and ideals which saw this institution through its pioneer days continue to prevail.

Under this appeare following news story:

BAKER-BOYER READY
FOR ADDED SERVICE

Officials of the Baker-Boyer National Bank stated today that no change whatever in the policies of their bank was necessitated by the temporary closing of the city's two other banks.

They have completed plans for rendering the additional services required by the community during the period needed to reorganize the other institutions, the statement added.

Last financial statement of the Baker-Boyer bank showed it to be in a strong condition. It has never at any time required notice of withdrawal and is recognized as one of the state's strongest financial institutions.

The same sound and conservative policies which have governed the institution's operations in the past will be maintained and continued, officers said.

Baker Boyer knew that its financial footings and liquidity were solid and that some customers couldn't go a week without cash, and so the bank's "do no harm" allegiance to its clients took over.

What happened next was a story that Jon Bren, current secretary of the bank's board of directors, learned from Ron Tomlinson, a past board member and previously the president of the former Bank of Commerce in Milton-Freewater. "He'd done some research, and what we discovered was that during the Great Depression, in the crux of that liquidity crisis . . . [the bank] asked all the Baker family members to contribute U.S. Treasury bonds to shore up the capital," said Bren, who joined the bank in 1977 and retired in 2012 as head of its trust and investment management services. "And that was something that was never known because the legend had it, after Franklin Roosevelt declared the bank holiday in 1933, we were doing business out the back door. This was because the family essentially decided this bank was worth fortifying."

Still, the level of public fear during the era remained palpable and easily could spark runs on banks and exacerbate problems without cooler heads prevailing. It was what President Roosevelt was trying to address when in his 1933 inaugural speech he told the nation, "The only thing we have to fear is fear itself."

Clubb related a story with a similar fear-not thread that she heard from Ned Lange, a former Baker Boyer board director. Lange's father was a doctor whose office was on the second floor of the bank.

"His dad had heard a whiff of what was happening down in the lobby, where people were starting to gather with questions" about the safety of their money, Clubb said. "He basically came storming into the lobby and, with a very hallowed voice he said, 'Where can I deposit this hundred dollars?' It kind of offset what was happening and actually had a very positive influence."

Three-quarters of a century later, echoes of the Great Depression returned when a financial collapse

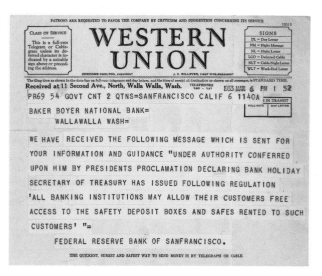

Telegram from the Federal Reserve notifying Baker Boyer of the President's declaration of a bank holiday in 1933 and the Secretary of the Treasury's requirement to allow access to safety deposit boxes despite the order to close the banks.

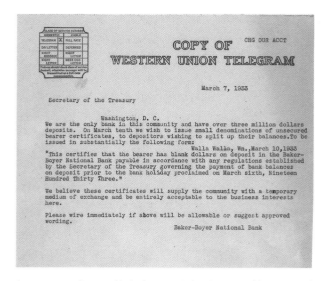

In response to Roosevelt's declaration, Baker Boyer quickly organized a plan to issue certificates of deposit for its clients to help them through the bank holiday, backed up by its $3 million in deposits. Ultimately, the Federal Reserve rejected the request.

Previous page: A transcript from the February 14, 1933, Walla Walla Daily Bulletin *notes Mayor Frank H. Richmond's proclamation declaring a two-month bank holiday for two local banks during the Great Depression. It is followed by an editorial and news story that Baker Boyer Bank was allowed to remain open due to its sound financial health and practices.*

in 2008 launched the Great Recession. Eight years into her tenure as the bank's president, Clubb was confronted with a major test of her leadership. It wasn't that Baker Boyer was on shaky ground. Instead, it was fear of the unknown: How bad will things get in the financial industry before stability returns?

"When you think of just how close the country came to falling into times like the 1930s," said Clubb, a Whitman College graduate who received her MBA from MIT's Sloan School of Management, "it was such a stressful time, a time that really challenged me from the standpoint of having to make some tough decisions."

RUINOUS TIMES RETURN

After the financial collapse that caused the Great Depression, the government enacted federal loaning and investing safeguards. These safeguards remained in place for several prosperous decades. In the 1970s, however, a 30-year trend of gradual deregulation got underway with urgings from the financial industry and with support from successive presidential administrations and congresses.

By the mid-2000s, unchecked greed and competition for market share had set the stage for the nation's worst financial crisis since the Great Depression—the 2008-2010 Great Recession. Its underpinnings were in a housing boom generated by a decade of gradually lowering mortgage interest rates, ever decreasing lending standards, and a commensurate rise in the market value of housing, drawing more people to buy homes not only as a place to live, but also as a nest egg to build money for their retirement.

The need for people with low credit scores to get access to credit spawned a new type of mortgage: subprime mortgages. As its name implies, these mortgages were for the riskiest of borrowers who couldn't buy a house with traditionally prudent mortgages.

"These subprime mortgages were toxic to both the borrower as well as those who bought them as investments once they were bundled together into subprime mortgage 'funds,' called collateralized mortgage obligations (CMOs)," Clubb said of the subprime loan packages. Baker Boyer early on understood the ethics and risks of subprime lending, unlike some other banks operating in Walla Walla, and refused to get involved in the scheme.

She recalled Judy Hicks, at the time head of residential lending, seeing what was going to happen when loans would be readjusted and saying, "This is insane. You don't make these kinds of loans. It's not the kind of product that is good for the clients. We're not going to do that."

At the same time, Clubb added, the bank's business banking manager, who later became the chief credit administrator, Russ Colombo, was seeing loans being made on Main Street commercial spaces with prices that could not be justified based on income from the property. "So again," Clubb said, "our competitors were giving a product that set their clients up to fail."

Clubb said Baker Boyer was criticized by many customers as "conservative" and "stodgy" when they sought subprime loans from the bank and were turned down.

"Is that conservative or is that prudent?" she said. "In my family it's been taught that it's prudent. We didn't overextend people."

Additionally, Baker Boyer did not purchase any subprime mortgages in its investment portfolio. "The goal of the portfolio of the bank is to have conservative investments—meaning we expect a return on our money," said Mark Hess, chief operating officer in charge of Baker Boyer's portfolio.

"The complex subprime derivatives not only failed to benefit us but also the communities we serve. We chose never to invest in them."

THE BIG FALL

The subprime house of cards began to collapse when the Federal Reserve started raising interest rates in 2004 to slow the economy and cool inflation. In two years, the prime rate went from 1.25 percent to 5.25 percent. When borrowers' initially low-rate subprime mortgage loans came due for adjustments to a much higher market rate than they expected as well as principal payments, they started defaulting in significant numbers.

The rising prime rate also slowed housing purchases, making it difficult for brokerages to sell the homes they foreclosed on. Their losses mounted as default rates increased along with their obligations to hedge funds, and other investors. Banks then stopped lending to brokerages, and dozens went bankrupt.

The first shock that kicked the crisis into high gear was the failure of Lehman Brothers—the fourth-largest U.S. investment bank, and a bank deep into derivative loans—which filed for bankruptcy on September 15, 2008. Mark Kajita, then head of investments for the Asset Management Division at Baker Boyer, was in New York as the crash precipitated. Frequently a guest commentator for Fox Business, CNBC, and Bloomberg, Kajita was now being asked what was happening on Wall Street. If Lehman could fail, which other big investment houses would be next and where would it end, market watchers and economists asked.

The answer came the next day, on September 16, when global mega-insurance company AIG—whose financial products arm had devised and sold credit default swaps, which insure investment products like subprime mortgage packages if they fail—had hemorrhaged to the point where it sought and quickly received an $85 billion rescue loan from the

On January 22, 2008, the British newspaper Metro reported steep losses in world stock markets and fears of a global recession.

Federal Reserve in an effort to confine the crisis. But panic in the industry had already set in as the depth and breadth of "toxic assets" held by major banks began to emerge.

The aftermath of the collapse of the housing market and subsequent failure of subprime loans was that investors, banks, and other financial institutions sat on their money, affecting lending across the economy because no one knew how insidious the subprime lending scheme had become in economic sectors and everyone was worried about which domino would fall next.

RESTORING ORDER

Realizing that more intervention was required, U.S. Treasury Secretary Hank Paulson and Federal Reserve Chairman Ben Bernanke on September 20, 2008, proposed that Congress authorize a $700 billion program to help the financial industry clear its books

THE CAUSE OF THE GREAT RECESSION

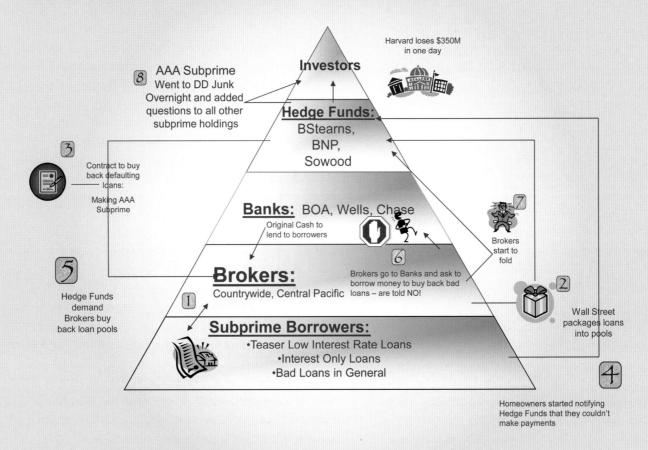

Harvard loses $350M in one day

Investors

8 AAA Subprime Went to DD Junk Overnight and added questions to all other subprime holdings

Hedge Funds: BStearns, BNP, Sowood

3 Contract to buy back defaulting loans: Making AAA Subprime

Banks: BOA, Wells, Chase
Original Cash to lend to borrowers

7 Brokers start to fold

5 Hedge Funds demand Brokers buy back loan pools

Brokers: Countrywide, Central Pacific

6 Brokers go to Banks and ask to borrow money to buy back bad loans – are told NO!

1

2 Wall Street packages loans into pools

Subprime Borrowers:
•Teaser Low Interest Rate Loans
•Interest Only Loans
•Bad Loans in General

4

Homeowners started notifying Hedge Funds that they couldn't make payments

The Rise and Fall of Subprime Lending

THE GENESIS OF the subprime lending crisis was the low-interest-rate environment that fueled speculation in the housing market.

1. Future homeowners with low credit ratings and little ability to pay back loans craved the opportunity to purchase homes as investments or as dream homes. However, they didn't have the financial stability to do so.

2. Mortgage brokers satisfied this need by creating a new type of loan, a subprime mortgage with minimal credit-rating requirements and extremely low-interest-rate-only payments for the first few years. When the introductory "teaser rate" time expired, the loan would revert to a regular mortgage with much higher interest rates and required principal payments, often tripling the mortgage payment.

3. Brokers used investment firms to package thousands of these loans into subprime mortgage "funds," and then sold shares in these "funds" to hedge funds, other investors, and particularly banks. Banks used their clients' deposits to purchase these subprime mortgage shares. The caveat was that if too many of the loans in the "fund" defaulted, the brokers were contractually obligated to purchase the loans back. In addition, companies like AIG sold insurance in case of default to investors.

4. When the housing market cooled, homeowners started notifying the owners of the subprime mortgage "funds" that they could not make payments on their houses after the mortgages transitioned to a principal and higher interest payment.

5. Owners of the subprime mortgage "funds" then notified the mortgage brokers and demanded that the brokers buy back the loans that were defaulting. They also insisted that AIG and other insurers honor their insurance contracts.

6. Mortgage brokers did not have the funds to buy back the defaulting loans. They approached banks to borrow money to do so, but were soundly denied.

7. Mortgage brokers started to go bankrupt and to fail to honor their commitments to buy back defaulting loans. Insurance companies, like AIG, were overwhelmed by the insurance payments required to pay the subprime mortgage "funds" owners. This left owners of the subprime mortgage "funds" without anyone to repay them for the mounting number of defaulting loans.

8. Owners of the subprime mortgage "funds" were faced with huge losses in the value of their investments. Owners included charitable foundations, hedge funds, and many banks. Banks were especially vulnerable because they were not able to sustain the losses with their existing capital. Many banks faced certain bankruptcy, leaving millions of depositors without funds to live day-to-day. These depositors included major corporations, such as GM, GE, and many others, who could not borrow money to meet their payroll and vendor obligations.

of toxic securities. The plan aimed to restore bank liquidity and loosen credit. Yet Paulson and Bernanke knew it would be bitter medicine that would be hard to swallow.

"It's a terrible situation to be in," Paulson said at the time in a televised press conference. "The only alternative is worse"—another long-term depression.

Their so-called Troubled Asset Relief Program, however, was shot down in the House of Representatives on September 29. Members argued that "bailing out" big businesses that had acted irresponsibly would be rewarding bad behavior. It was a feeling shared by a large segment of the public, many of whom protested in the streets with signs saying, "Bail out people, not the banks."

The immediate result of the House's bipartisan refusal, however, deepened miseries when the stock market plummeted 777 points, the largest single-day drop in its history at the time. That shock spurred the Senate to pass its version of the bill. This bill, unlike the House proposal, infused capital into banks accepting the bailout. It also included new regulatory oversights, payback requirements, and help for homeowners at risk of foreclosure. The House went along with that new plan and President George Bush signed the TARP Act on October 3, arresting the immediate crisis and opening doors to a way out of the morass. The TARP plan had provisions requiring institutions to pay back the federal money they accepted, with interest— which in ensuing years resulted in an overall profit for the U.S. Treasury.

But it would be many months before the financial tsunami unleashed its most destructive forces, echoes of which lingered for years as the crisis rippled from Wall Street to Main Street. Foreclosures had put many Americans out of their homes and deeply in debt after exhausting their savings. Homeowners who had traditional fixed-rate mortgages, including those who paid them off, watched their home values plummet, not to return to their previous levels for years. Consumers who saw their stocks and retirement investments decline in the crash tightened their belts. All of which affected the manufacturing and retail sectors, forcing production cutbacks and layoffs that in turn rocketed the national unemployment rate to 10

Mark Kajita, here featured in a Bloomberg financial news telecast, was tapped by CNBC and other national networks for his expertise during the recession.

percent. In Walla Walla County the jobless rate shot up from a respectable 4.3 percent in October 2008 to 9.8 percent by January 2010. The county would not see a 4.3 percent rate again until September 2017.

At Baker Boyer Bank, Clubb knew she was in for a rough ride as president and CEO when she learned Lehman Brothers had failed and that other large banks might follow, or worse. She had an immediate decision to make: what to do to protect Baker Boyer's liquidity and its customers' access to cash. Normal practice was for Baker Boyer to put its excess deposits in a larger national commercial bank to earn interest. But these were not normal times: banks couldn't know for sure if the larger banks they invested with were sound. "You are faced with making a decision that could easily be deemed so foolish," Clubb said. "Like, are you seriously going to put millions of dollars of your excess deposits at the Federal Reserve Bank, earning zero percent interest?"

Yet that is what Clubb decided to do as preparation for a worst-case scenario, though not without a lot of self-examination and discussion. "I've always been a superconfident person and I've always been a very optimistic person," she said. "And I think I've always been one to be bold and make choices that do not follow the pack. But this particular choice just felt like it was potentially a reaction where you're letting your emotions drive you to unjustified fear."

She also weighed her choices with Mark Kajita, then the bank's Asset Management vice president. They were both leaning strongly toward the Fed option. Besides putting excess deposits at the Fed, Kajita decided he would also move client investment cash balances to the Federal Reserve if the situation worsened, even if it violated trust regulations in force at that time.

Megan's father had died a few years earlier, so for a final opinion, she called Vernon Kegley, the bank's president from 1982 to 1985. "I laid it all out there and said to him that I feel like I need to put the money at the Fed. And he just validated immediately that that was the right thing to do," she said, adding that the ability to draw on the knowledge of past or retired employees is a valuable tool for navigating through unusual situations. As it turned out, Baker Boyer's parking of excess deposits with the Federal Reserve at no interest lasted only a few days, when the Fed reversed policy and started paying interest in an effort to provide liquidity for banks and to get them to extend credit to stave off a deepening of the crisis.

CALMING THE HOME FRONT

Clubb recalled watching a news channel showing a crowd of people at a North Carolina bank, Wachovia, demanding their deposits be returned in the summer of 2008. She knew this was the risk she had to protect the bank from. Having surmounted her own fears and doubts, she knew she and others at the bank had to do the same for clients and the community, even though Baker Boyer did not deal in subprime loans and would not need to accept TARP funds. Sensing that a storm was brewing, "that summer we began to focus our advertising on Baker Boyer's strength," said Clubb.

When the greed and recklessness of the subprime scheme began to be exposed in the media in the weeks and months after the crash, a natural skepticism about the financial industry in general turned into anger, distrust, and outright cynicism. Depositors and investors where Baker Boyer operated in the Walla Walla Valley, the Tri-Cities, and the Yakima Valley were no different.

"I could see what was evolving out there, and I had never lived through a period of time in my life where there was a sense that there could be a run on a bank," Clubb said. "As seen in the 1930s Depression, when financial markets stumble it causes this panic that exacerbates the problem tremendously. And if you had to say what were some of the main contributing factors to why the recession got so deep in both cases, it's the human psyche. Fear can slip the entire financial system into a tailspin."

In an effort to stem the potential for a local panic and a run on the bank, Clubb, Kajita, and other bank executives mounted a confidence-building communications blitz with clients and the community at large, to lay out causes of the recession and assure clients and customers that Baker Boyer Bank remained strong and was at no risk of failing.

"That required us first of all to focus on making sure our employees had confidence that we were sound—that we knew how to get through times like these, that we were well positioned from a financial standpoint to survive," Clubb said. "If they didn't understand our unique strong position and have trust, there was no way we were going to get that sense of confidence to the clients and the community."

She recalled a lunch she and Kajita had with a community member who had lost faith in his investments. "He was basically saying, 'We ought to just sell out. We've got to sell.' It was at a time when things were already way down, so it would have been the wrong time to sell. But again, drawing on the experience that we had, we were able to talk someone off the ledge of making the wrong choice at absolutely the wrong time."

Peter Allen, the bank's executive vice president who oversees the Wealth Management division and a sixth-generation Baker family member, recalled another meeting he and senior portfolio manager Ted Cohan had with a client who had grown frantic about her investments.

Top: Vernon Kegley was Baker Boyer's president from 1982 to 1985.

Bottom: Four presidents of Baker Boyer gathered for this April 2014 photo. (From left) Mark Kajita, Megan Clubb, Vernon Kegley, and Stephen Kimball.

"She had seen her account go down by $20,000 a month and was completely convinced that it was going to go down that much every month until it was gone," Allen said. Cohan tried to explain mathematically how that's not how markets work. "I swear she almost came over the table at him," Allen said. Eventually they convinced her that if she got out of the market she would never recover her losses. "So at that time we were able to keep that client in the market, and of course then the market started to turn, and it wasn't quite so scary anymore."

Indeed, the community confidence in Baker Boyer engendered by presentations that Clubb and others held resulted in a major increase in deposits from people who banked elsewhere in town.

"The world goes to hell in a handbasket and our deposits are growing," said Hess. "People to this day remember banks that took TARP. There was no reason for us to take TARP. We had plenty of capital and it wasn't going to be eroded with problem loans and bad investments."

Said Clubb: "Just before the crisis, Baker Boyer was holding $350 million in deposits for our clients. As the crisis deepened and people became more concerned, our deposits jumped more than $50 million in 18 months. Deposit growth of this size was unique, and it demonstrated how much confidence our clients had in Baker Boyer's strength and survivability." Ten years later, Baker Boyer's deposits were at $529 million.

FEELING GRATEFUL

It could have been nightmarish for the economy, however, had Paulson and Bernanke not made the tough choices they did to keep the nation from descending into a full-blown depression, Clubb said. "They, literally, saved the country, in my opinion, from an even greater, more disastrous situation."

Sensing trouble ahead in the nation's financial sector, Baker Boyer began running ads in the spring of 2008 to assure people the bank was on solid footing. This May 2008 ad featured a Great Depression era quote from Oklahoma cowboy, humorist, and social sage Will Rogers.

Ironically, it was perhaps fortuitous that Bernanke, a Princeton University economics professor before serving on the Federal Reserve, had studied the causes of the Great Depression for his doctorate thesis. In a lecture on economic policy at Washington and Lee University in 2004, four years before the Recession hit, he noted several failures by the government as well as the Federal Reserve that, if they had acted otherwise, might have limited the financial calamity of the 1930s.

In May 2010, Clubb met Bernanke in Washington, D.C., when she was training after her appointment to the Federal Reserve's regional office in Portland. She told him about the Treasury Department's 1933 telegraph that Baker Boyer received ordering the temporary closure of all U.S. banks, and how alarming and stressful it would have been had she received a similar order in 2008.

"I'm so grateful I didn't receive one of those," she recalled telling him. "And I said, but you probably hear from all sorts of people how thankful they are. And he looks at me and chuckles and says, 'No, not so much.'"

"He and Paulson did some really brave work, in my opinion," Clubb said. "It was a situation that you don't find yourself in very often, but all you have are undesirable choices that nobody approves of. They will criticize choice A, choice B, choice C. You don't have any choices that someone would look at and say, 'That is a really good one.' But the status quo, do-nothing option would likely have sent the country back to where we were in the 1930s."

Megan Clubb, who served as a director with the Federal Reserve Bank of San Francisco, met Federal Reserve Chairman Ben Bernanke in Washington, D.C., in 2010.

BAKER BOYER PRESIDENTS

Dorsey Syng Baker
(1869-1888)
founder

John F. Boyer
(1889-1897)
brother-in-law of DSB

Miles C. Moore
(1898-1919)
son-in-law of DSB

W.W. Baker
(1919-1948)
son of DSB

N.A. Davis
(1948-1956)*

Dorsey S. Baker
(1956-1965)
grandson of DSB

Baker Ferguson
(1965-1982)
great-grandson of DSB

Vernon D. Kegley
(1982-1985)*

Stephen G. Kimball
(1985-2000)
great-great-grandson of DSB

Megan F. Clubb
(2000-2014)
great-great-granddaughter of DSB

Mark H. Kajita
(2014-present)*

*Not a member of extended Dorsey Syng Baker family

CHAPTER 3

Charting New Waters

"When you have been around for 150 years and your goal is to be around for at least another 100—when you're talking about a quarter of a millennium—the impossible is possible, the improbable is probable, you just have to plan for it." — Mark Kajita

A hundred and twenty years ago William "Wee Willie" Keeler was tearing up big league baseball with his bat. At 5 feet, 4 inches and weighing 140 pounds, he was one of the smallest players in the game. When he retired in 1910 after 19 seasons with Baltimore and Brooklyn, he had amassed a career batting average of .345 and an on-base percentage above .400. Asked for the secret to his success, the diminutive Hall of Famer said his motto was simply "Keep your eye on the ball and hit 'em where they ain't."

Fast-forward to 2005, the year Harvard Business School Press published *Blue Ocean Strategy*. It's a book that Baker Boyer president and CEO Mark Kajita often refers to when talking about how the bank maintains its edge by bucking a several-decades trend of financial institutions growing larger and more impersonal through mergers and acquisitions.

In a synopsis written for a 2015 update to the book, global business strategists W. Chan Kim and Renée Mauborgne contend that success comes not from battling competitors but from creating "blue oceans"—untapped opportunities ripe for growth. The alternative

Illustration of Baker Boyer Bank by employee Brittany Nelson of Walla Walla, 2019.

The Whitman Hotel and Baker Boyer Bank in the heart of Walla Walla.

is to remain in "a bloody red ocean of cutthroat competition" that results only in rivals fighting over a dwindling pool of profits.

Or, if Wee Willie were around and asked to write the synopsis, he'd likely say that success comes when you aim for holes in the playing field where the competition "ain't."

Baker Boyer has successfully sailed competitive waters for 150 years by sticking to its vision of being a true community bank that believes its health is tied directly to the economic health of its local businesses, depositors, and investment and loan clientele. Unlike banks immersed in the expansion trend, Kajita said, "We don't have to grow just to grow; we just have to make sure we are evolving fast enough to meet the needs of our community."

That relationship "is where we were founded, and we never lost track of that," Kajita said. "If you're lending to a client and you know you're going to make a lot of money, but in the end you're going to bankrupt the client, that's unforgivable. I think a lot of banks now are so focused on short-term profits, quarterly profits, that they're not focused on a hundred years from now. . . . Their philosophy is just so different from ours.

"In the 1970s, '80s, and even into the '90s the industry was all about growth: getting more deposits, getting bigger, and eventually buying out other banks," Kajita said. But, he added, that's not the way Baker Boyer wants to operate, "because if you do that, you're going to become a super-regional and lose the fiduciary trust you have with the community.

"The essence of fiduciary responsibility is that your interests are never above the interests of your client or community," said Kajita, "even if it's at the expense of yourself. That is fiduciary. And that is what Baker Boyer has done for 150 years."

The "red ocean" of banking nowadays, according to Kajita, is seen in the increase of multistate regional banks. They may market themselves as community banks because they have a branch in town, but deposits and receipts are sent to headquarters where loan, investment, and operating decisions are made by strangers from afar.

A December 25, 2017, article in the *Wall Street Journal* lends credence to Kajita's thinking. It reported that the expansion of banks branching into other regions and states is making it harder for small communities to maintain and develop their businesses. Citing federal data, the article reported that 625 of the nation's 1,980 rural counties didn't have a locally owned community bank, twice the number in 1994. In addition, at least 35 counties had no banks at all, while approximately 115 were served by one branch.

Larger banks are "gravitating" toward making bigger loans. They have fewer ties to local communities, often rely on algorithms to gauge creditworthiness, and are "less likely to have the personal relationships that have helped local bankers judge which borrowers were a good bet."

"The phenomenon, almost automatically, is getting worse," the article stated. "Bankers say they don't see enough business in small towns. Small towns say bank closings make it harder to do business."

Kajita, a frequent commentator on Bloomberg and CNBC financial broadcasts, noted that "in essence, the financial industry has lost its way" in its focus on immediate profits instead of nurturing long-term stability in communities. "When you bring in super-regional and national banks, especially with Internet banking, you're taking deposits from one community and investing them in another," he said. "I think that's why you're seeing so many problems with bigger banks. They're struggling to find a model that respects community. I think the model is moving back to community fiduciary responsibility."

That model, Kajita said, is based on a simple, long-held axiom in community banking: "What is good for the long-term health of the community is good for the long-term health of the bank."

In his letter to shareholders in the bank's 2018 annual report, Kajita encapsulated his beliefs on the subject with the Latin term "cui bono"—who benefits. Between a community and its bank, benefits are never mutually exclusive—success for both comes in a symbiotic manner that is mutually beneficial.

In its 150 years of banking through hard times and good, Kajita said in his letter, six generations of Bakers and the bank's family of employees "have never forgotten that our success is born only after the communities we serve succeed."

Megan Clubb and Mark Kajita in the bank's 2018 annual report. It included a letter from Kajita to shareholders highlighting the principle that when customers and clients succeed, so does the bank—encompassed in the Latin phrase cui bono, who benefits?

LETTER TO SHAREHOLDERS

Cui Bono
BY MARK KAJITA

In Latin, "who benefits?" In the relationship between a community and a bank, it is never mutually exclusive. Sucess happens when it is mutually beneficial.

1   2018 Annual Report

HOLDING THE BATON

BAKER BOYER HAS BEEN on *Seattle Business* magazine's list of "Washington's 100 Best Companies to Work For" for 13 consecutive years—the most of any company in the state—and ranked on *American Banker* magazine's Top 200 Community Banks list since 2008. "This is one of the things I am most proud of," said Megan Clubb, who led the bank from 2000 to 2014. "I inherited an incredible legacy based on the foundation of leaders who came before."

Former president Stephen Kimball credited Baker Boyer's success to a team approach. "I love Andrew Carnegie's quote," said Kimball: "No man will make a great leader who wants to do it all himself or get all the credit for doing it." During his 15 years of leadership—or as he put it, "holding the baton"—Kimball said, he was fortunate to have great help.

President from 1985 to 2000, Kimball worked closely with two other former presidents, Vern Kegley and Baker Ferguson. "Baker Ferguson and other senior people were extremely wise," said Kimball. "Vern is a good example of a strong non-family influence on the bank. He contributed a lot to the bank's success."

Kimball also attributes the bank's success to client satisfaction and operational excellence. "We are a small town bank deeply rooted in family history displaying a high standard of business practices for six generations."

Megan Clubb and Peter Allen, Baker Boyer's executive vice president of wealth management, accept Seattle Business magazine's award naming the bank the "Best Family Business" in Washington in 2012.

Baker Boyer has received recognition through numerous local, regional, and national awards, including:

» *American Banker* magazine, Top 200 Community Banks (2008-present)

» *Yakima Valley Business Times*, Best of the Valley, Best Financial Advisor, 2015

» *Seattle Business* magazine, 100 Best Companies to Work For, 13-time honoree

» *Seattle Business* magazine, Best Family Business Award, 2012

» *Walla Walla Union-Bulletin*, "Best Bank" (2004-2019), 16th consecutive year

» *Walla Walla Union-Bulletin*, "Best Mortgage Lender," (2016, 2017, 2019)

» *Walla Walla Union-Bulletin*, "Best Financial Advisor" (2014, 2015)

Sailing Into "Blue Oceans"

Before leading Baker Boyer as a fifth-generation family member, Megan Clubb worked for a global consulting firm that helped CEOs and executives of its client businesses solve strategic challenges. She used that training and led her Baker Boyer team through a multiyear strategic planning process. The result was to move Baker Boyer in a new direction that had at its foundation team-based collaboration and financial consulting for clients seeking professional wealth management.

"Looking back to the '80s, we were order takers and our clients had to navigate to each area of the bank to figure out what they needed and who to talk to," said Susie Colombo, now a vice president and family advisor, who worked closely with Clubb in early 2000 to reinvent the approach. "We were empowered to create a client experience that we all knew was the correct path for us, the bank, and especially our clients."

In short, the concept is akin to building a round table for clients surrounded by investment, lending, financial planning, tax, and legal experts all talking with each other in their client's behalf. It's a departure from the way a person seeking wealth management is typically advised—separate visits with each professional at his or her specialty's firm, who were unlikely to be talking with other professionals about their mutual client's personal needs and hurdles.

To Kajita, who practiced as a certified public accountant in Walla Walla when Clubb discussed her team approach with him, it was "revolutionary" and pivotal in his decision in 2003 to accept her offer to join the bank as an investment portfolio manager. "When I was a CPA at Thompson & Kreitzberg and at Ernst & Young working with very high net worth clients, it became apparent that CPAs saw their

Mark Kajita, 2003.

clients once a year and attorneys saw them even less," Kajita said. "But no one was helping their clients day-to-day, walking them through some very difficult decisions. No one had the time to explain information to them in a way they could understand."

When Clubb asked him to join the bank, "we clicked," he said. "We understood what this vision was going to be 20, 40, 50 years from now. Megan gave me the power to make a difference. That's why I'm here. At big accounting firms, you're a small cog, and you aren't necessarily able to take an idea and execute on it. At Baker Boyer, it isn't about individuals; what we're really good at is taking eight or nine really smart people as a team and coming up with an executable plan and a vision."

Having been empowered by Clubb, Kajita in turn made it his mission to empower clients as well with sound financial literacy and decision-making abilities. He recalled reading an article in which Apple cofounder Steve Jobs was asked how he created the company and came up with his wildly popular Macintosh computers, iPods, iPads, and iPhones. "And Jobs said, 'I started with the experience I wanted the user to have and then I worked backward to what the technology would be to make the person feel that way.'"

"And I think that is so appropriate," Kajita continued. "If you start off with wanting people to feel empowered, you work backward from that. Who do I need to hire; what kind of experts will clients need? Will the experts be able to communicate well? Can they speak at a level that brings this very complex subject down to everyday discussion? Who will people feel comfortable opening up to? Once you got to that, the team of experts, that's the core."

After several years of offering the team approach to banking, investment, and trust clients, in 2016 Baker Boyer branded its service D.S. Baker Advisors.

Advisors have various expertise in law, taxes, loans, investments, wills, accounting, financial planning, trust and estate management, business succession, and other fields. How many and which experts to be assigned to a client depends on the nature and complexity of the client's needs and wealth goals. As advisors, they cannot by law execute legal, tax, and other financial decisions for clients, but clients can incorporate their team's advice and bring it to the client's lawyer, CPA, or other professionals to act on.

Accounts are managed with customer relationship management software the bank customized. "We built a system so everybody connected with a client can come together and build that client's journey—where they've been and where they're going," Kajita said. "Everyone now has a vested interest in making sure they are meeting their goals."

It all begins for clients with a few initial interviews in a deep, personal discussion about themselves and why they're seeking help. The objective is to learn of any unspoken "elephants in the room," which might include personal or family issues that pose major obstacles or potentially result in clients making emotional rather than practical decisions.

"A client has to go through this financial therapy before we can know how to help," Kajita said. "For many clients this is a shock because they were used to 'OK, I'm coming to talk to you, you're going to give me your spiel, and you're going to ask me to invest money or take a loan.' Our policy is 'Give us a chance to understand who you are, what your intent is.' Then once we understand that, we'll respond with 'Here's how we think we can help.' Or 'We're not sure we can help you, but here's another company that can.' That's been a hallmark of ours as well. We don't sell anything; we present options and let them choose."

Rob Blethen, as manager of D.S. Baker Advisors' Family Advising team, conducts intake interviews and helps form specialist teams for

D.S. Baker Advisors services pamphlet.

each client. "The family advisor is like the front of the relationship," he said. "We figure out who they are at their core, then their goals short- and long-term, and then we use our financial planning department and internal and external experts to figure out the best plan for them, and finally, we help them orchestrate that plan over a period of years, updating frequently to serve them for decades.

"We ask questions they often haven't previously explored. Questions that make a big difference for their future. Then we offer expert guidance and advice. Like structuring an investment portfolio that will give them security in retirement. Providing a loan structure that is tailored to safely grow their unique business. Directing them to their legal advisors with issues involving their wills. Helping them navigate through challenging family dynamics as they face the tough task of passing their business to the next generation," he said. And so it goes, with some clients needing only one advisor to help them with a simple decision, while others have highly complex finances that require a full platoon.

"Before we made these changes, people would say we were a bank with some really good consultants," Kajita said. "And I always corrected them and said, 'We're actually a consulting firm that just happens to have banking powers."

New Frontiers

Another evolution in Baker Boyer has been a gradual expansion of its physical presence in Walla Walla and other communities in the region sharing common economies and needs. "It's not that we don't expand, but we have to know what the goal of the expansion is," said Kajita. "If it is to help strengthen the economy of the community, and we see how we can make a huge difference, we'll move in."

In 1986, Baker Boyer acquired the Bank of Commerce in Milton-Freewater when the family that owned it wanted to sell and approached Baker Boyer. Only 12 miles south of Walla Walla but still in the valley, it presented a ready-made opportunity to extend operations in an agricultural community sharing common values with its larger neighbor to the north.

"Acquiring the Bank of Commerce was a way for us to continue to serve the valley," said Clubb. "The farm community in the valley is inclusive of the Oregon side of the valley and the Walla Walla side. It is a community of people who all know one another. We really are neighbors."

In 2001 the Bank of Commerce was consolidated under the Baker Boyer name in a new branch building.

"If you start off with wanting people to feel empowered, you work backward from that. Who do I need to hire; what kind of experts will clients need? Will the experts be able to communicate well? Can they speak at a level that brings this very complex subject down to everyday discussion? Who will people feel comfortable opening up to? Once you get to that, the team of experts, that's the core."

— Mark Kajita

WALLA WALLA'S FIRST DRIVE-THROUGH BANKING

Baker Boyer Bank opened its first branch in Walla Walla's Eastgate shopping area in 1958, offering the first drive-through banking service in town.

Inset: W. E. Rawson, first manager of Baker Boyer's Eastgate Branch, looks on as Virginia Henry (formerly Virginia Kelly) checks a transaction envelope Rawson handed her at the drive-through window. Seated is Henry's daughter Debra (Kelly) Parsekian.

In the early 2000s, amid the trend of larger banks swallowing up smaller ones, an interstate mega-bank acquired a Pacific Northwest regional bank. It closed its trust and wealth management offices in the Tri-Cities, moving that function to its regional office across the state in Seattle.

Jon Bren, who was heading Baker Boyer's trust and wealth management division before he retired in 2012, saw the pullout as an opportunity to provide the bank's personal team approach to another nearby community with economic underpinnings and commerce similar to Walla Walla's. Baker Boyer for years had been working with trust attorneys in the Tri-Cities. "I've always thought that in an area where you have a need for service and no competitors, you have a pretty good chance for success," Bren said, adding that the Tri-Cities trust operations had roughly $100 million in client assets under management. After Bren presented the opportunity to the board, space was leased in a Kennewick building and Baker Boyer hired the staff of the former bank. When it opened, Baker Boyer acquired about 20 percent of the value of the trust accounts from clients who didn't stay with the departing bank.

"But then," Bren continued, "just six or eight months into that, a very significant estate came along in which we were named executor and trustee. So that really was a turning point in terms of profitability and the viability of that office."

Lightning struck again about a year later, when the same opportunity arose in Yakima with a pullout by the same interstate bank's trust office there, stranding a number of clients who wanted a more local, personal touch handling their accounts.

"And that probably was even a bolder move," Bren said. "We were unknown, but we did have trust services which other banks didn't and we could provide a local trust officer. And again, it could have failed, but fortunately there was a small group of estate planning attorneys and accountants in Yakima and the Lower Valley who were affiliated with Whitman College or had a Walla Walla connection. They knew about Baker Boyer. And I have to say that our success today there was largely based on that group of professionals who kept referring business to us."

Newspaper advertisement for the Bank of Commerce.

The Tri-Cities branch was first housed in the iconic "Flashcube Building" in Kennewick.

Baker Boyer broke ground in March 2019 for its $10.5 million financial management center in Yakima. This was the bank's largest building project since it built its seven-story Walla Walla headquarters in 1911.

Many of those referrals were multigenerational Yakima Valley farm families that played major roles in developing the area into a global leader in orchard fruits and hops production. "Today," Bren said, "we have a client list of about 20 significant Yakima families, and have built a real presence and image."

Indeed, the welcome that Baker Boyer has received in Yakima coupled with the success of the Yakima venture allowed the bank in March 2019 to break ground for construction of a $10.5 million, 19,000-square-foot financial management center in the city to be complemented with a full team of D.S. Baker Advisors. It marks the bank's largest building project since it built its seven-story Walla Walla headquarters in 1911. The facility, to open in 2020, also will include a community space to be available for business and nonprofit events for up to 100 people. The room is intended to help bring people together to discuss how to bring changes to the community and, said Kajita, "in the end, to help make the Yakima economy stronger."

Peter Allen, who became the bank's trust and wealth management chief following Bren and Kajita,

sees more growth in store for the Yakima operation. "We manage about $250 million and we started that branch in 2002," he said. "And there's certainly more opportunity there that we haven't tapped."

Symbiosis Equals Success

In the early years of post-Great Depression deregulation, bank mergers, and acquisitions, Kajita said, "Baker Boyer was criticized for holding true to our core beliefs and not expanding fast enough, or in a way other financial institutions had grown. Many of those institutions have failed or have been merged into other financial institutions. However, Baker Boyer remains and is stronger than ever." In his 2018 shareholder report, he said it was "the most profitable year in the history of Baker Boyer."

Apart from a few territorial Walla Walla Valley farms still in family hands, Baker Boyer remains the oldest commercial enterprise in the region and the oldest bank in the Pacific Northwest. And like the children's story "The Little Engine That Could," Baker Boyer has always been the little bank that could—and did—surmount its challenges by sticking

Bank offers help for furloughed federal workers

Baker Boyer is offering unsecured credit for those employees affected by the shutdown.

By VICKI HILLHOUSE
of the Walla Walla Union-Bulletin

Baker Boyer Bank is responding to the federal government shutdown with a new personal loan program for furloughed employees.

On what is the first official payday most of the estimated 800,000 federal employees will miss since the furlough began Dec. 21, Baker Boyer today rolls out its initiative to offer assistance.

The "We've Got Your Back Program" extends unsecure credit based on one month's net pay, up to $10,000, with simplified qualifying terms, the Walla-Walla-based bank announced. The move puts the community bank in the company of a number of other businesses offering relief to those affected by the shutdown.

The program is designed to help affected federal workers make payments on bills such as mortgages, child care, food and other essentials, Baker Boyer President and CEO Mark Kajita said.

"Having been a child of parents who worked as federal employees, I know how financially difficult times can get when there is a federal government shutdown," he said in an announcement.

The service is available to those within the geographic footprint of Baker Boyer (Walla Walla Valley, Columbia Basin and Yakima Valley) who are

See **BANK**, Page A6

Front-page story in the Walla Walla Union-Bulletin on January 13, 2019.

WE'VE GOT YOUR BACK

ALTHOUGH EXERCISING SUCH care has been, and remains, a constant when Baker Boyer loans money, "there's always been a trust in the bank that we will do the unconventional," said President and CEO Mark Kajita.

Doing the unconventional while practicing the bank's mantra of "do no harm" came together on December 22, 2018, when President Trump ordered a partial shutdown of the federal government over a congressional impasse on funding the U.S.-Mexico border wall. Kajita, other executives, and the bank's board of directors quickly devised their "We've Got Your Back" program, offering affected federal employees no-fee, income-based loans of up to $10,000 to help them pay their bills. The terms were bare bones: zero percent for six months with an option to extend up to 12 months at 3 percent fixed. The program was announced on January 4, 2019, and Baker Boyer was one of the first banks in the nation to offer the help.

Borrowers did not have to be regular bank customers; they had only to show they were furloughed without pay, be subject to a credit score, and live within Baker Boyer's areas of operation in the Walla Walla Valley, Columbia Basin, and Yakima Valley.

"We are lending cash at half of what we can make on that money through standard loans and investments," said Kajita. "Because if we don't, the community in the end will be hurt. Through no fault of their own, our downtown businesses and restaurants will be hurt. The bank is in a unique position to add comfort to people who are uncomfortable." Kajita, a child of parents who were federal employees, said he knew how difficult living can get with no paychecks.

The shutdown lasted 35 days, more than two federal pay cycles, ending on January 25, 2019. "We've Got Your Back" ran 30 days beyond that.

LEGACY GIVING PROGRAM

SINCE ITS INCEPTION in 2016, Baker Boyer's Legacy Giving program has given away $248,000, and according to Peter Allen, Executive Vice President of Wealth Management and a sixth-generation Baker family member, that's just the beginning. "It's a start," said Allen, "but I believe we will be giving away a lot more."

The impetus behind the program is to provide funding to help kick-start major community projects that will have an impact for generations. "Our Legacy Giving program was created to empower people and organizations in the community; to help them make a change for a stronger community," said Mark Kajita, President and CEO of Baker Boyer.

Projects selected as grant recipients include the new teen center in Walla Walla for at-risk youth called The Hub, the Cancer Survivorship Project at Providence St. Mary Medical Center, the Center for

Women and Children at the Christian Aid Center, the Learning Center at the Walla Walla YMCA, the new aquatic center at the Yakima YMCA, and the community meeting room at the new Blue Mountain Action Council facility.

In addition to the grants awarded through the Legacy Giving program, in 2018 Baker Boyer gave over $150,000 to 178 organizations supporting community nonprofit and civic groups, programs, and events. The company takes a multifaceted approach to giving back to the community. "We have a resource that far exceeds any monetary gifts we can give the community," said Allen. "We have 180 people who can pitch in and give their time to something they are passionate about."

Employees at the bank are encouraged to find a cause they care about and get involved, and they do not have to sign off of the company clock to attend nonprofit board meetings and community fundraising events. The goal is to allow employees to be fully engaged in making a meaningful contribution and not worry about missing work. "I feel pretty strongly about that," said Allen. "They still have to do their job, but we want part of their job to be supporting causes they care about that benefit the local community."

As a Baker family member, Allen is committed to continuing the legacy of supporting the whole community. "That's an expectation that has been built in for generations of the Baker family," said Allen. "It's part of the deal. And that's a good thing."

Baker Boyer President Mark Kajita (fourth from right) presents a ceremonial check for $25,000 to help build a new aquatic center at the Yakima YMCA.

to its founding "do no harm" principles and maintaining fidelity with its customers, clients, and community.

The bank as a whole, through its loans, investments, and donations, and its generations of Baker family members and bank employees who contributed their personal time and money, has remained in a constant symbiotic collaboration with the communities it serves. That combined force turned their once remote valley in the undeveloped Pacific Northwest into a preeminent center of agriculture, education, arts and culture, wine, and tourism.

Kajita cited a finding from The Aspen Institute, a multidiscipline, nonpartisan think tank for values-based leadership based in Washington, D.C. In a report identifying factors that influence economic growth, long-term stability, and prosperity for local communities, he said, Aspen "reiterated what Baker Boyer has known for 150 years. Social and economic growth and equity is not just altruism, but financially it is just good business. These goals are not mutually exclusive, but intricately intertwined for long-term success.

"When you have been around for 150 years and your goal is to be around for at least another 100—when you're talking about a quarter of a millennium—the impossible is possible, the improbable is probable, you just have to plan for it," Kajita said. "We are doing so not by wringing every last penny of profit out of our communities but by looking for ways to grow the communities we serve."

Community volunteering by employees, from the top executives on down, is a big part of Baker Boyer's corporate culture, as seen in this effort at Blue Mountain Action Council's food bank warehouse in 2019.

ROSENDO GUIZAR— HOMEGROWN LEADERSHIP

Rosendo Guizar, 2003.

LOOKING BACK ON the arc of his life and career, Rosendo Guizar considers himself perhaps the most unlikely person ever hired to work in a bank's loan department.

"I was probably the least qualified candidate," he recalled, when he responded in 1996 to a newspaper ad for a commercial loan assistant job at Baker Boyer. If the bank job didn't come through, he said, his other option was to keep an appointment in two weeks with a U.S. Air Force recruiter in Spokane.

However, when the interviewer asked him for any final thoughts, he recalled saying, "I'm sure you have much more experienced people applying for this job, but

I can guarantee you one thing: If you hire me you will never regret the decision."

Today, 23 years later, Guizar is the bank's vice president in charge of credit administration. He oversees the bank's entire commercial and consumer lending portfolio, assesses and manages credit risks for the bank as well as clients, and helps set lending policies and practices.

"Next to being president, it is the most critically important job," said Megan Clubb, chair of the board and former president and CEO.

RAISING HIS SIGHTS

In the late 1960s Guizar's father left his position as a laborer in a rural logging camp in Michoacán, Mexico, to work on farms in the Yakima Valley. After three years of seasonal work he landed a job with the Charvet hop ranch near Grandview, and a place on the property where he could bring his family north to live and gain citizenship.

"I grew up in the Yakima Valley pretty much my whole life," Guizar said. Despite working demanding farm jobs growing up, Guizar maintained good grades at Grandview High School, even tutoring other students. The school librarian, Darcy Ahlquist, took note of this smart, industrious youth and

asked what he planned to do after high school.

"Really, my aspirations were just to get a job indoors," he said. "I remember thinking pretty vividly that working as a cashier or something at Safeway would be a pretty good step up." But Ahlquist believed Guizar could set his ambitions higher and encouraged him to apply to college.

Ahlquist was so motivated to realize Guizar's potential that she drove him 75 miles to Walla Walla to attend Whitman College's open house. "I owe everything to her education-wise. My parents were hard workers but they never went through school; it wasn't really a priority."

He received a full scholarship from Whitman and graduated in 1994 with a degree in biology and chemistry.

BLAZING A PATH TO SUCCESS

Once he was at the bank, Guizar's drive to learn, grow, and advance was in full gear. He gave himself 18 months to work as a loan assistant to become competent in the art, practices, business needs, and seasonal cycles of commercial lending, and then he would shoot for a full loan officer position. But nothing opened up.

Sensing his frustration, his boss suggested Guizar draft a proposal to create a new position, along with research data on how it could generate enough revenue to cover the bank's expenses for his pay and benefits. His view of the bank's lobby from his office, and noticing that "hardly any Hispanic people come in," gave him an idea to help bridge a cultural gap.

"My parents grew up distrustful of banks—why are they there, what's in it for them—they didn't have the idea that you could actually have a relationship with a bank," he said. So Guizar drafted a proposal to move from the commercial to the consumer lending department, which would put him in direct contact with people needing car, home, and other simple, non-business-related loans. And he included his fluency in Spanish as an asset. The bank quickly approved his plan and his promotion.

"I was off and running," Guizar said. He soon went from seeing few Hispanic people in the lobby to people waiting a half-hour or more near his desk for him to finish up with one customer and get to them.

Eighteen months later, when a loan officer position finally opened up in commercial lending, Guizar applied after much "soul searching." At the time there weren't many Hispanic-owned businesses in Walla Walla.

WISDOM COUNSELOR

The challenges for Guizar as a commercial loan officer were getting to know the various business sectors, which were safe bets and which were risky, and how the bank could help clients mitigate risks in order to receive a loan. He also needed to learn about his clients, the economics of their types of businesses, and how some succeed on solid footings while others limp toward failure. All of which served as tools for him to succeed over the next 20 years and earn his promotion in January 2018 as the bank's chief credit administrator.

"You don't necessarily have to know how to run the business, but you do have to know how to interpret the financial numbers and equate it to what's going on in the business," Guizar said. Sometimes that requires having brass-tack conversations with clients when Guizar spots "red flags" in business practices that could result in not renewing a line of credit or worse, bankruptcy. The bank wants to make a loan, but not if doing so will hurt the client.

"If someone comes back to you after you've turned them down, I know I've done the right thing—it

Rosendo Guizar, a vice president, became in charge of credit administration in 2018.

wasn't a humiliating and degrading experience," said Guizar. "If I had been the type of person to sit here and pour cold water all over your dreams, you'll never come back to the bank." Guizar's goal is to protect the bank and the client, by offering business advice that could set the client up for future lending goals.

"It's a very rewarding thing; you become a counselor and a sounding board. And that's what we all aspire to," said Guizar.

CHAPTER 4

Building Bountiful Legacies

More than 20 Percheron horses pull a combine operated by a five-man crew harvesting wheat near Touchet in Walla Walla County in 1923.

> *"It is great to be working with the land, as well as the people and local businesses that understand the challenges and opportunities within local agriculture."*
>
> — Nathan Rea

As Dorsey Syng Baker's mercantile in Walla Walla was evolving into a bank in the 1860s, the entrepreneur had another venture in mind that helped propel wheat farming to a grand scale in Washington.

Growing grain in the Walla Walla Valley started when Marcus and Narcissa Whitman established their mission in 1836 and planted wheat seeds they'd brought with them from the East. This marked the first cultivation of wheat between the Cascade and Rocky Mountains. By 1841, the Whitmans were milling their own flour.

As settlers traveling the Oregon Trail began arriving en masse in the mid to late 1850s, a patchwork of wheat fields sprang up in the valley's fertile lowlands. Baker arrived in Walla Walla in 1859 to start his mercantile, but soon elevated his sights to the hilly drylands above the valley to see if they, too, might support crops.

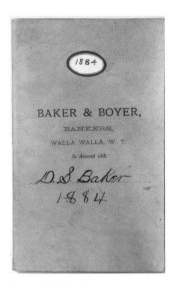

Dorsey S. Baker kept meticulous records on his wheat acreage in the Walla Walla area. This personal ledger was for the year 1884.

Before engine-driven combines it took a lot of energy from horse and human alike to harvest wheat in the Walla Walla Valley's rolling hills.

"At that time it was the general opinion that the hill lands, and especially those not adjacent to the mountain range, were fit only for pasturage," W.W. Baker wrote in *Forty Years a Pioneer*, a 1934 book about his visionary father's business ventures in the Pacific Northwest. "These lands . . . only supported a growth of bunchgrass indigenous to all of the drylands of the Inland Empire."

Having previously farmed and built flour mills in southern Oregon, Dorsey Baker had a notion that would put that "general opinion" to rest. In the early 1860s, he bought 5,000 acres of mostly government hill land rising above Walla Walla Valley a few miles north of town.

"His friends questioned his views with reference to these soils, asking him why he purchased drylands when he was free to pasture stock on the millions of government acres" extending from Idaho west to the Cascades, W.W. Baker wrote. "But he had other visions for its use."

He sectioned the land into three tracts. The largest, with a creek flowing through it, was left as pasture. The two east tracts were fenced and the ground was plowed. His first crop was flax, which did not require the wheat-growing practice of leaving newly exposed ground open to air and rain for a year to allow native grass roots to decay.

W.W. Baker's father "produced a fair crop the first year," he wrote, with flax in following years becoming "quite an export product" for use in manufacturing oils on the coast. His achievement proved to himself and doubters that the upper drylands—with average precipitation of 17 inches a year—could grow crops without irrigation. He then planted a successful wheat crop. In a few years he went beyond the valley into the rolling drylands of the Palouse country north and east of Walla Walla and bought large tracts to grow wheat. So did more farmers.

"It is known as forty-bushel land," W.W. Baker wrote of the crop yields, "but at times has produced sixty bushels per acre."

By 1864, wheat harvests in the Walla Walla area were feeding several flour mills in the town. More settlers arrived in the 1870s and '80s and fanned out across the Palouse into what are now Columbia, Garfield, Asotin, Franklin, Adams, Whitman, Lincoln, and Spokane Counties. They planted wheat. The success of dryland wheat farming in an area with an average rainfall of less than 27 inches was no longer in doubt. Today wheat ranks as the number one field crop grown in Walla Walla County, and number three in Washington. Statewide production in 2018 of 153.2 million bushels was valued at $691 million, according to the Washington Grain Commission.

TREES OF PLENTY

The Walla Walla Valley was the first area in the territory to be settled by indigenous people. It also takes credit as the cradle of Eastern Washington's expansive tree fruit industry. Along with wheat, the Whitmans had planted a 50-tree apple orchard at their mission when they arrived from New York in 1836. Orchard fruit production became a local industry in the 1860s as settlers arrived in the valley. The new orchard farmers were soon followed by tens of thousands of gold seekers roaming northeast Washington, Idaho, and Montana. They used Walla Walla as a provisioning hub and a place to spend winters.

In his 1978 book on the history of Walla Walla County horticulture, Joe J. Locati, a Walla Walla native and retired Washington State Department of Agriculture inspector, reported that the earliest known commercial orchard was planted on a ranch east of Walla Walla in 1859. That same year the first nursery providing fruit tree rootstock was established south of town along Yellowhawk Creek. More nurseries and orchards were planted in ensuing years. Though exact figures are sketchy, Locati did reference early historian Frank T. Gilbert as stating that the County Assessor in 1874 recorded 1,238 acres planted with fruit trees that year. Production was enough to meet local demand, with surpluses in volumes worthy of marketing elsewhere.

The Yakima Valley expanded into orcharding even faster and began to overtake Walla Walla County in orchard fruit production in the 1880s. The first known orchard in the Yakima Valley was planted at a Catholic mission established in 1852. It was located on Ahtanum Creek, south of what would become the city of Yakima. Settlers soon arrived. Those who attempted farming in the dry climate could grow tree fruits in the volcanic soil with added irrigation from the Yakima River, and its tributaries, flowing from the Cascade Mountains.

This undated photo, looking west toward the Cascade foothills on what is now Yakima's Nob Hill Boulevard, shows the degree to which fruit orchards dominated Yakima County's farm economy, even in the horse-and-buggy days.

West from Nob Hill.
Yakima Valley, Wash.
Smith.

CROP ACREAGE

In a 2013 Port of Walla Walla report on leading crop acreage in the county, the 180,000 acres devoted to wheat dwarfed all other crops. The acreage of other top crops, besides tree fruit and wine grapes, included hay (13,500), potatoes (11,000), corn (7,700), processing peas (7,000), and barley (4,400).

Above: Dr. Nelson G. Blalock started his Blalock Fruit Company in 1897. It was one of the largest orchard operations in the Walla Walla Valley. In 1915, about the time this photo was taken, the packing warehouses and wholesaling operation were sold to Paul H. Weyrauch, who changed the company name to Blalock Fruit and Produce Company.

Orchard planting began expanding rapidly in the 1870s when several private canal and ditch companies built small-scale irrigation systems. With the arrival of the Northern Pacific Railroad, and its access to national markets, a partnership started construction of the Sunnyside Canal irrigation project. The system fed 42 miles of ditches and laterals by 1892, and 700 miles by 1905.

Until then, Yakima County had been leading the state in sheep and hop production, the latter of which began in 1872, when a settler planted cuttings he brought from New York. By 1910, the county produced more apples than any other county in the nation, a ranking it still held in the U.S. Department of Agriculture's most recent industry census, in 2012. Yakima County now has 84,000 acres of orchards. Walla Walla County's current tree fruit acreage now stands at approximately 12,500 acres. Tree fruits, mostly apples and cherries, also are a major commodity in the Milton-Freewater area, with approximately 3,200 acres.

Valley crop diversity on smaller scales also includes garbanzos, alfalfa, and Walla Walla Sweet Onions. The trademarked onion is grown only in the valley and is prized by gourmands nationwide, and in 2007 by legislative decree became Washington's official state vegetable.

CONNECTING TO THE WORLD

In the territorial days, getting crop surpluses to markets elsewhere was a challenge in the vast, undeveloped Pacific Northwest.

One option was the Mullan Road from Walla Walla to Fort Benton on the Missouri River, which had been officially completed

in 1862. It provided a wagon- and pack-train route to ship grain and other merchandise to Idaho and Montana gold-mining camps and settlements along the way. But when the mines were depleted in a few years, the demand fell.

In 1867, eyes turned to Portland. Some wheat had been sent down the Columbia River on steamboats to the Pacific port and loaded on ships to English ports for distribution in Europe. However, the first 32 miles of that journey—the road from Walla Walla to the Oregon Steam Navigation Company's docks on the Columbia at Wallula—posed a troublesome hurdle. The dirt route was deeply rutted from years of stagecoach and wagon traffic bringing people and merchandise to the town. At times it was impassable due to weather, and the hauling fees that teamsters charged farmers were expensive.

What was needed, farmers and business owners saw, was a railroad to handle the increasing volume of crops. And thus began Dorsey Baker's last great enterprise, a seven-year effort that was fraught with funding and construction complications.

Dorsey's adventure commenced in 1868 with a group of prominent citizens incorporating as the Walla Walla & Columbia River Railroad Co. They elected Baker as president and began seeking funding and project cost estimates. Shares were sold to 24

stockholders, who were assessed payments as needed as construction proceeded. Later that year, Congress granted a right-of-way through public lands to build the railroad. The grant also permitted the county to aid construction with a loan, provided it was put to voters in a bond measure. The measure required a 75 percent majority to pass. The election was to be held in November 1871.

Trouble began when the bond failed by 18 votes. The next year, 19 of the two dozen stockholders did

The Walla Walla was the first of several Porter, Bell & Company steam locomotives Dorsey S. Baker bought for his Walla Walla & Columbia River Railroad Co. It was used to help build the narrow-gauge railroad from Wallula to Walla Walla and to haul freight.

WALLA WALLA'S FAMOUS ONION

THANK A FORMER French soldier and Italian immigrants to the Walla Walla Valley more than 100 years ago for introducing what is now Washington's official state vegetable: the Walla Walla Sweet Onion. While you're at it, tip your hat to a Japanese-American family for helping to keep the local industry thriving amid growing global competition.

Peter Pieri is credited with bringing seeds of an onion prevalent on the island of Corsica to Walla Walla when he immigrated to the region around 1900, after his discharge from the French army.

Peeling back layers to the local origins of the trademarked onion was an undertaking of Joe J. Locati, son of an Italian who immigrated to Walla Walla in 1889. Locati wrote *The Horticultural Heritage of Walla Walla County, 1818-1977.*

Italian immigrants at the time dominated gardening and noted the onion's ability to winter over in its young stage of growth. They also found that the valley's low-sulfur soil gave the onions a sweet, mild flavor without the pungency of other strains—and afforded an experience without the tears when peeling or chopping them.

John Lucarelli stands on the running board of an early 1940s Ford truck laden with sacks of sweet onions harvested at the Tony and Rhea Lucarelli Farm in 1947. The onion field was on the corner of Blalock (Spitzenburg) and Campbell Roads near Walla Walla.

"Its succulence comes from its own nature, the rich, loam soil—and the Walla Walla growers' techniques," Locati wrote. "There is no other onion quite like it that I know of. And connoisseurs agree."

The onion's popularity spread over the years and at one time it competed only with Georgia's Vidalia sweets. The name was trademarked in 1995 under a U.S. Department of Agriculture ruling to prevent sweet onions grown outside the valley from co-opting the brand.

The local onion's 90 percent moisture content, however, made its shelf life short. And when consumers in the early 2000s started demanding sweet onions year-round, other areas around the nation and in South America began developing their own strains. The market competition and volume resulted in a slow decline of Walla Walla acreage—from about 1,400 at its height in the 1990s to about 600 in 2019—as several small farm families got out of the business.

But local growers like Mike J. Locati and the Hamada family are determined to hold the line. Locati's family started Locati Farms in 1905. The Hamada family came to Walla Walla to farm after World War II. They had lost their land in Western Washington when Americans of Japanese descent were sent to internment camps during the war. Together, Locati and the Hamadas started Walla Walla River Packing and Storage in 2003, and then built it into a consortium of local growers to process and ship Walla Walla Sweets to major grocery chains throughout the West and in British Columbia.

Harry Hamada, general manager of the business, which partnered with a national fruit and produce marketing company, said local growers representing 450 acres in the valley are in the consortium and selling their onions to Costco, Fred Meyer, Albertsons/Safeway, and other major outlets. "If you want to go out and play with the big boys," Hamada said, "you've got to produce."

Rhea Lucarelli (left), husband Tony (seated on the truck bed), and workers take a break while loading sacks of sweet onions at the Lucarelli Farm's onion field near Walla Walla. Rhea Lucarelli worked at Baker Boyer as a bookkeeper from about 1955 to 1985.

This railroad track anchoring spike was used on the Walla Walla & Columbia River Railroad Company rail line.

Walla Walla & Columbia River Railroad Co. (WW&CRR) locomotive.

not pay or were delinquent in eight assessments the company required.

"Either they had lost faith in the enterprise, or their private affairs took precedence in the distribution of their cash resources, which resulted in a complicated condition of the company's finances," W.W. Baker wrote.

But Dorsey Baker and the remaining stockholders—among them his bank partner, John F. Boyer, and former mercantile manager William Stephens—were in it for the long haul. Part of the urgency was Baker's sense that the Union Pacific would soon be branching into the Northwest and along the south bank of the Columbia River to Portland. It had completed its transcontinental railroad from California to the East in 1869. Baker wanted to build a spur that would link the Walla Walla Valley to the national rail network.

Baker now realized he would have to put up much of his own money. He also envisioned a pay-as-you-go plan, with the railroad starting to earn money when the first leg of construction east from Wallula reached its first station in Touchet, about half the distance to Walla Walla. At no time, however, would he consider taking a loan from his bank or using deposits for the financially risky project, W.W. Baker wrote.

The initial project estimate the company received reportedly topped $700,000 for roadbed construction, standard rails, lumber for ties, two locomotives, several freight cars, and other equipment and labor. Quality timber for the rails, ties, and trestles was sourced from forests along the upper Yakima River near what is now Ellensburg, and floated in rafts to the Columbia River to a mill the company would build near Wallula. Baker saved expenses by constructing a narrow-gauge railroad that handled smaller locomotives and building the cars from scratch using purchased wheels. Another unusual cost-saving measure reflected his ingenuity: they constructed the rails with wood stringers surfaced with strap iron that could be replaced later with solid metal rails if the project proved profitable.

Porter, Bell and Co. in Pennsylvania agreed to build the first of two locomotives Baker ordered for $4,400. Freight cost totaled $1,424 for shipment around the tip of South America to Portland, then up the Columbia River to Wallula by the Oregon Steam Navigation Co.

The first locomotive arrived in Wallula in June 1872. The mill company on the Columbia River, run by Baker's eldest son, Frank, produced its first ties in November, when the work of grading the rail bed, building trestles, and laying track began in earnest. For Baker, it involved periodic four-day trips on horseback to the Yakima River logging camp and twice-a-week rides to Wallula to check on progress—

not a comfortable proposition for a 49-year-old, partially paralyzed man who also had a bank to oversee.

By 1874, construction—employing many of the estimated 500 Chinese laborers and craftsmen in the valley at the time—had progressed the 16 miles to Touchet. There, the train took on its first wheat shipments and helped pay for further construction. The previous year without the railroad, wheat and flour shipments from the valley to Wallula amounted to 570 tons. With the railroad, 4,021 tons of grain and flour—a 700 percent increase—plus another 1,126 tons of merchandise, were hauled.

"With this favorable outlook before him, [Dorsey Baker] found comfort in the thought that he might be able to purchase and pay for the balance of the rail to complete the road," W.W. Baker wrote.

The 20 miles of heavier regulation rails arrived from Europe by the fall of 1874, and by the following May all the wood and strap-iron stringers—which wore excessively in sharp curves and steep grades—were scrapped and replaced. Construction also progressed to Lowden Station, completing 22 miles.

THE FINAL STRETCH

The cost of grading, ties, and rail to finish the remaining 10 miles to Walla Walla, however, worried Baker. Work continued a few more miles to Whitman Station, then halted eight miles out of Walla Walla. The company had a $75,000 debt due for the new rails, and more were needed for the final stretch. Rather than delay until more money could be earned hauling freight from the existing stations, Baker and company directors proposed that the city of Walla Walla and its citizens invest $75,000 in company stock to complete the project within a year.

An appointed citizens committee rejected the amount and suggested a compromise of $20,000. Baker came back with a final offer: $25,000 plus rights-of-way for nine miles and acreage in the city to build a depot. Fearing that if the end of the line was at Whitman Station, a rival town might be established around it, the committee accepted the offer. The project was completed on October 23, 1875, making the Walla Walla & Columbia River Railroad Co. the first railroad company operating in Washington Territory. The total construction cost was $323,715, roughly what Baker had estimated he could build it for with his cost-cutting plan.

In 1876, its first full year of shipping from Walla Walla to Wallula, the railroad hauled 15,266 tons of export grain—wheat, barley, oats, flaxseed, and flour. Wool and miscellaneous merchandise amounted

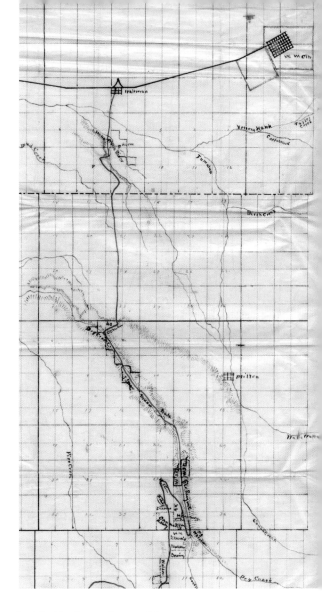

The blue line at the top of this 1879 map drawn by Dorsey S. Baker shows part of the east-west route of the completed WW&CRR track into Walla Walla. The red line shows the planned north-south route from Whitman Station in Walla Walla County south to the Blue Mountain foothills in Umatilla County, Oregon.

Passenger and freight rates charged as of August 1876 by the WW&CRR.

WW&CRR passenger pass for Levi Ankeny signed by Dorsey S. Baker in 1878. A businessman and politician, Ankeny lived in Walla Walla and served as a U.S. Senator from 1903 to 1909.

to another 4,034 tons. Those annual totals, respectively, grew to 37,664 and 11,644 tons by 1879.

There is no record of total revenue generated over those years and from which station, but the railroad charged $5 a ton to haul freight the 32 miles from Walla Walla to the river. Before the start of construction, teamsters were charging $13 for that same haul.

In 1877, Baker began two spurs. The first ran from Whitman Station south to the Blue Mountain Station to serve wheat and orchard farmers across the border in northern Umatilla County. The second ran east from Walla Walla to the town of Dixie to haul lumber from the Blue Mountains and wheat from the foothills.

Neither spur was completed under Baker's ownership of the railroad. As he had foreseen, the transcontinental Union Pacific was extending its lines from the south into the Pacific Northwest, and the Northern Pacific was building a route from the Great Lakes that would cross Washington from Spokane to Seattle. He knew it wasn't in his best interests to compete with a national rail line to be built along the Oregon side of the Columbia to Portland. Thus, in January 1879, he sold six-sevenths of the railroad's stock shares to the Oregon Steamship Navigation Company, and held on to the remainder and his role as president.

Later that year, the Oregon company was acquired by Portland business mogul Henry Villard, along with other transportation companies, in an amalgamation called the Oregon Railroad and Navigation Company. In October 1879, Baker sold his final shares in the railroad he'd built largely with his own money to Villard. Villard gained controlling interest in the Northern Pacific Railway and then formed a new entity called the Oregon and Transcontinental Company. In 1881, it converted the Walla Walla line's narrow-gauge rails to standard gauge to meet the Northern Pacific line being built east from Portland to eventually connect with the Union Pacific Railway's national network.

"This was Doctor Baker's last undertaking, his health having failed him soon after completion of [his] road," Miles C. Moore wrote in a 1903 article for the Oregon Historical Society. Moore, a son-in-law of Baker, was the last territorial governor of Washington and later the third president of Baker Boyer Bank. "Perhaps no man in the Northwest," he wrote, "has left his name more completely entwined into the history of his chosen country and city than has Dorsey S. Baker . . . whose fortunes were the fortunes of the town, and whose successes were the success of the place he called 'home.' "

FARMING THEN AND NOW

If you were farming in the early days of Walla Walla, you might go to Dorsey Baker's mercantile and pick up a "foot burner," a single-blade plow you'd tether to your ox, mule, or horse and follow behind to till the soil.

If you were raising wheat, you'd need a header, a contraption with spinning horizontal blades. You'd also need a team of livestock to push it through the field to lop off the kernel-bearing heads onto a belt that would drop them into a wagon following alongside. The wagon would carry the heads to a stationary machine called a thresher to knock off the kernels—literally separating the wheat from the chaff. Several horses attached to each end of poles linked to a driveshaft powered the thing by walking in circles. Steam-powered threshers came along in the 1880s.

By the 1890s, you'd have the labor-saving advantage of a new mechanical behemoth called a combine, to be drawn through the field by a sturdy team of horses, sometimes several dozen, on hilly terrain. It was a heavy machine that came by its name because it combined the heading and threshing operations as it cut wide swaths of grain.

D.S. Baker ordered a six-wheel locomotive, the Blue Mountain, from Porter, Bell & Co. in Pittsburgh in 1877, for his narrow-gauge Walla Walla & Columbia River Railroad. It joined three other Porter locomotives of various wheel configurations. In January 1879, Baker sold his railroad to the Oregon Steamship Navigation Company, which in turn was bought in July 1879 by the Oregon Railway and Navigation Company. Thus, the O.R.&N. Co. lettering marks the locomotive's cab.

But then, as now, productive, profitable farming has always required further technological, scientific, and economic innovation.

Engine-powered combines and tractors came along after World War I, some with leveling systems that would prevent them from overturning on steep slopes. By the 1930s, the need for a great deal of four-legged power was a thing of the past for those who could afford modern equipment, which then included combines that could cut a seven-foot swath at a speed of three miles per hour. Combines nowadays are far larger and faster, with 45-foot cutting heads and speeds of about five miles per hour. They are accompanied by bank-out semi trucks that haul the harvested grain directly from the combine to shipping storage sites.

Innovation to deal with changing economies and markets also has kept the valley's agricultural industry thriving. When the price of wheat fell during the Great Depression and a Canadian tariff closed the valley's main market for fresh peas and other fruits and vegetables, Walla Walla responded in 1932 by opening its first cannery. Others soon followed and by the mid-1940s more than a dozen canneries were operating in the valley. But advances in refrigeration technology would make storing and shipping frozen and fresh produce to global markets more economical, and canneries had all but disappeared in the valley by 2005.

Science has also played an increasing role in farming efficiencies and meeting environmental concerns. In the late 1940s and 1950s, the advent of soil science provided a big boost in crop production. Through the analysis of soils at agricultural universities and labs, farmers could determine which nutrients were needed for specific crops and apply fertilizers accordingly to increase yields.

In more recent years, science has brought solutions to lower the input costs of pest controls. An early example was the development in 1988 of a fungus-resistant strain of soft-white wheat. The predominant wheat crop in the Northwest and the region's chief farm export to Pacific Rim countries in Asia, it's prized for making udon noodles, sponge cakes, and other pastries. Reduced chemical use in fighting wheat fungus saved $30 million in five years.

Agricultural science researchers also have developed grain strains that produce higher yields with the same ground moisture. John Mathwich, Baker Boyer Bank vice president and senior trust advisor, was born in Athena, Oregon, and raised on a family farm started by his grandparents. A 1978 Oregon State University graduate in agriculture resources and economics, he said his alma mater and Washington State University researchers frequently introduce new grain. "They've got some varieties that

This 1898 scene eight miles out of Walla Walla shows a 16-horsepower "advanced" traction steam engine (left) and a thresher (right) used to separate kernels from cut wheat. Before the days of combines that both cut and threshed wheat in one pass, it took quite a bit of equipment to harvest fields. Some equipment was made locally, such as this thresher.

Dr. Nelson G. Blalock's mammoth steam tractor draws a train of wagons with nearly 800 schoolchildren from Walla Walla to the county fair in October 1890.

are better in certain areas than others," he said. "Last year we had some grain in the foothills that was yielding 140 bushels to the acre. Thirty years ago, 100 would have been a dream."

Technology-driven practices to save money on fertilizer and other inputs—as well as control soil erosion and protect groundwater and streams—have also come to the forefront. Until the 1990s, preparing fields required separate passes over the field to till the soil, seed, and fertilize. That has since been reduced by no-till planting with rigs that punch through the surface with a drill to deposit seeds and fertilizer in a single pass. That approach is now routine for more than half the cropland in the state. Benefits include lower fuel and tractor-maintenance costs, and better retention of precious ground moisture.

State-of-the-art computerized yield monitors and GPS field-mapping systems mounted on combines also are cutting input costs, in a practice called variable rate seeding and fertilizing. Part of an overall trend of precision farming, this approach begins with the previous harvest as the combine's system maps the field and records spots where yields were good and where they were less so. "When you go to seed that field, it will show you that this area over here only produced 40 percent of the average," Mathwich explained. "So the next year when you're in there, you'll put in less seed and less fertilizer because you know that the plants aren't going to be there that can take that up. There is an environmental benefit of not putting that excess on there, but also it's an economic efficiency."

Modern-day wheat harvesting in the Walla Walla Valley. A large combine (left) with a full hopper prepares to convey the grain to the truck following alongside for hauling to a storage facility, as a second combine (right) cuts and threshes on another pass through the field.

Modern combines equipped with computers and GPS systems show and record various data about the field and yields as the machine harvests row by row, all accessible via the farmer's smartphone.

YAKIMA HOPS

THE ORIGIN OF THE Yakima Valley's hop-growing industry more than 150 years ago—and its staying power today as the nation's leading provider of the beer-flavoring ingredient—boils down to two names: Charles Carpenter and Bert Grant.

Hop historians credit Carpenter as the first to introduce hops in the valley when he settled in the Ahtanum Creek area in 1868, planting rootstock he'd brought with him from New York. The bines flourished in the valley's volcanic soils, hot, dry summers, and ample irrigation from snow-fed Cascade streams. More farmers started planting hops, and by 1876 the valley shipped 80 bales to brewers in Seattle and Portland.

When the Northern Pacific Railroad extended into the valley in 1884 and opened new shipping markets, acreage mushroomed. By the 1890s, the Yakima Valley was the center of hops in Washington, and in the 1960s it became the nation's leader in production.

Although the industry's chief market was major American brewers, beer-drinkers' tastes began to change in the 1990s toward liking more flavorful, spicier brews. And it was in Yakima that the nation's now ubiquitous craft-brewing industry was born, thanks to Bert Grant.

A Scottish-born Canadian, Grant was an international brewery consultant before settling in Yakima, where he started the Yakima Brewing and Malting Company. It was a small operation. He used more hops to provide body and flavors in his brew, something he thought major beer brands

A worker on a horse-drawn platform tends to rows of trellised hop plants in the Yakima Valley in this 1936 photo. The valley is the nation's leading producer of hops.

lacked. With his recipe popular among locals, he opened Grant's Brewery Pub in 1982 after convincing regulators that Washington law permits individual brewers to operate one place to make and serve their products direct to consumers. His pub thus became the first of its kind in the U.S. since Prohibition.

Grant died in 2001, but his style of beers and pub concept spread nationwide. Small craft brewers coast to coast seek out the more than 35 strains of hops produced in the Yakima Valley to make their distinctive ales, lagers, and stouts. Major brewers also noticed and added new lines of more hop-heavy beers. Yakima Valley hop growers now produce 75 percent of the hops grown in America and market them around the world.

This current view, northeast of Walla Walla, looks down onto a parcel of farmland originally owned by D.S. Baker.

Banking on Farm Legacies

The cost of competing with ever-larger farms has brought another change to local agriculture: small family farms calling it quits because their owners or heirs no longer want the struggles. Some sell, while others put their lands under farm management or in managed trusts or services like those Baker Boyer Bank has offered for more than five decades.

With an average of 65,000 acres of farm land under management—a small part of that in Oregon and Idaho—the bank in a sense is the largest farming entity in the valley. "We don't own the ground," Mathwich said, "but we may have management authority over the largest amount of ground in the county."

The service relieves owners of the day-to-day and year-round duties and responsibilities it takes to farm. The bank's farm managers lease the lands to active farmers seeking more acreage and ensure that crops are marketed, income is disbursed to clients and heirs, federal programs are managed, and taxes and bills are paid. Mathwich said, "They can work with us and feel confident that we're doing the best job for them."

Clients include both people who own or inherit land but don't live in the region and locals who want to keep it in production but not farm it themselves. "And a lot of times the owner is a trust," said Peter Allen. "So it's not a person but it's a trust for the benefit of other people, where they want to keep the farmland but nobody wants to farm it."

While some clients hold the land as an investment, Mathwich said, others "want to always own that land because of memories, the family ties." For sisters Lynne Bush and Jeanne Eagleson, fifth-generation Baker family members who live in Seattle and travel quite a bit, it is important to know their family land will continue to grow crops. "We want the land to be farmed and not built on," said Eagleson. The land is part of the original farmland belonging to D.S. Baker and has been in their family for the past 100 years, and managed by Baker Boyer for the past 40 years.

"It's the legacy," said Megan Clubb about Baker Boyer's farm management services. "It's establishing an opportunity for that legacy to continue."

Stanley Bishop, J.H. Rea, and John Hunt Rea pose in front of a diesel tractor on the Rea farm during pea harvest in 1950.

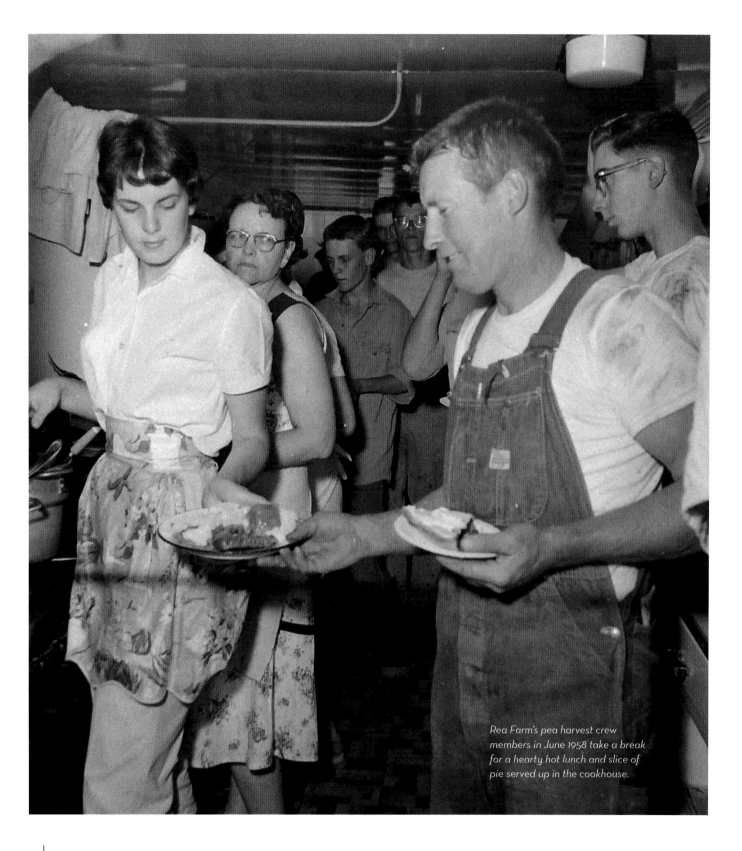

Rea Farm's pea harvest crew members in June 1958 take a break for a hearty hot lunch and slice of pie served up in the cookhouse.

GENERATIONS

At the base of the Blue Mountains, Nathan Rea stands in fields acquired by his great-grandfather John "Harris" Rea, who arrived in the Walla Walla Valley in 1903 on a train carrying mules from Charlotte, North Carolina. "We are very blessed to be right on the Blues," said Rea. "We have the opportunity to grow really good crops here."

The surrounding fields are planted with patented winter wheat seed crops known for high yields. Looking out over the field to the west Rea points out a wheat variety with French lineage called "Artdeco," to the south "Norwest Tandem," and the west a Syngenta variety "SY Dayton."

The land was not always planted in seed crops. In the 1930s to 1950s, Rea's great-grandfather and sons Harris Tremayne—or H.T.—and John Hunt raised peas for canning or freezing. It was a time of expansion for the family farm, and at the height of that era harvesting peas involved large crews, mobile cookhouses, and a 24-hour seven-days-a-week schedule.

As demand for peas declined, advancements in technology and planting equipment allowed the family to increase the amount of wheat in the crop rotation, and barley worked its way back into the planting cycle as well. Not only does barley offer a soil health benefit as a rotational crop in breaking the disease cycle, but it had recently opened the door to a new niche market.

In 2015 Rea partnered with Phil Neumann of Mainstem Malt as a grower for the specialty craft beverage industry. Mainstem Malt works with family farms in Washington and Oregon to grow premium malting grains that are Salmon-Safe certified. The third-party certification ensures agricultural practices that protect water quality, stream health, and biodiversity. The target buyer: brewers and distillers who want to make the perfect Northwest crafted beers and whiskeys for ecologically minded customers who

value supply-chain transparency—or just want to know where the grains in their favorite drinks come from.

All grain and malt under the Mainstem brand is sold in a single varietal, single farm, and single field format so brewers and distillers can develop flavor profile across variety, geography, and seasonality. Rea's 2016 hard red winter wheat is featured in Crossbuck Brewing's NoPac IPA. "It has made barley growing more exciting," said Rea, "and with more upside potential."

After studying agricultural business at Washington State University, Rea spent eight years working in Washington, D.C., as an aide for U.S. Representative Greg Walden, eventually serving as the Oregon congressman's legislative director. In 2013, he returned with his wife, Emily, a clinical psychologist, to work the family business, H.T. Rea Farming Corp.

"Agriculture is an amazing world that—like any business—has lots of complexities," said Rea. "The technology is going to go really fast. You have to be right on top of your game." His biggest equipment expenditure this spring was software upgrades on his John Deere tractors—paying to unlock codes to turn on more functions in the GPS-based system that sends real-time data to the cloud to map and monitor each field.

Adapting to changes in market demand, rapidly developing technology, farming practices, and ecological regulations is all part of running a profitable business. Rea likes to be proactive, whether it is trying something new like specialty barley or bolstering sustainability and conservation efforts to gain certifications that can open new markets. Bottom line, he wants to do what is right for the land and pass on the opportunity to farm to his children.

"It is great to be working with the land, as well as the people and local businesses that understand the challenges and opportunities within local agriculture," said Rea.

CENTENNIAL FARMS

THE WALLA WALLA Valley is rich with descendants of families that started farms in the territorial days before Washington became a state.

The Centennial Farms Project, commissioned by the state to commemorate its 100th anniversary, included a survey of farms established before 1889. Of the 412 farms recognized as Centennial Farms, 294 responded to a follow-up questionnaire in 2014 asking if the farm was still owned by the same family. Of the 51 Centennial Farms reported in Walla Walla County—second in the state to Whitman County's 82—at least 34 were owned by descendants of their founders.

"As a group, Walla Walla County's Centennial Farms are the oldest in the state," stated a report of survey. "More than half the county's farms were established before 1875," with the two oldest still in family ownership since they began in 1858.

Here is a list of the 51 state-recognized Centennial Farms in existence in Walla Walla County before statehood in 1889. The list indicates the year a farm was established. Whether a farm was still owned by the same family in 2014 is indicated by Yes, No, or No Response.

The Aldrich Farm, 1858, Yes
John P. Anderson Farm, 1883, NR
The Barrett/McInroe Farm, 1869, Yes
The Bergevin Farm, 1865, NR
James Berryman Farm, 1878, NR
The Coffin Farm, 1884, Yes
The Collins Farm, 1886, Yes
The James M. Cornwell Farm, 1868, Yes
The Cummins Farm, 1881, Yes
The Dement Farm, 1879, NR
The Drumheller Farm, 1877, NR
The Ferrel Farm, 1880, Yes
The Five Points Farm, Inc., 1884, Yes
The Flathers Farm, 1871, NR
The Fulgham Farm, 1886, Yes
The Gallaher/Buroker Farm, 1869, NR
The Gallaher/McInroe/Young Farm, 1869, NR

The Gilkerson/Davis Farm, 1863, Yes
The Hastings Farm, 1887, Yes
Philip Hoffmann, Sr., & Sons, 1884, Yes
Kenney Farms, Inc., 1866, Yes
The Robert F. Kibler Farm, 1870, Yes
The Lane Farm, 1889, NR
The Leid/Hansen Farm, 1889, Yes*
The Lloyd Farm, 1863, No
The Lowden Farm, 1883, Yes
The Lowden/Dodd Farm, 1869, Yes
The Thomas Lyons Farm, 1871, Yes
The Lyons/Dunphy Farm, 1871, Yes
The Magallon Farm, 1882, Yes
The Martin Farm, 1869, NR
The William McCown Farm, 1878, Yes
The McCulloch Farm, 1883, Yes
The McKinney Farm, 1864, NR

The Christian Miller Farm, 1888, Yes
Mission Farms, 1880, Yes
The Cyrus Nelson Farm, 1877, NR
The Pettijohn/Sanders Farm, 1881, Yes
The Pettyjohn Farm, 1858, Yes
The Plucker Farm, 1874, Yes
The Reser Farm, 1862, NR
The W.P. Reser Farm, 1868, Yes
The Roberts Farm, 1871, Yes
The Saturno/Breen Farm, 1880, NR
The Shelton Farm, 1869, Yes
The Strahm/Mason Farm, 1874, NR
The Struthers Farm, 1883, Yes
The Tompkins Farm, 1887, Yes
The Waggoner Farm, 1882, No
The Yeend Farm, 1870, Yes
Yenney Farms, Inc., 1872, Yes

Yes=34 No=2 NR=15 Total=51

* The farm is still owned by the same family but no longer includes any portion of the original parcel.

A full moon rises over farmland below the Blue Mountain foothills in the Walla Walla Valley, where commercial agriculture has been a leading industry since the mid-1800s.

View looking north across the Walla Walla Valley from L'Ecole Nº 41's Estate Ferguson Vineyard at the top of the hill, part of the SeVein Vineyards complex.

CHAPTER 5

Grapes of Wealth

"The founders were bound by a common belief that cooperation trumps competition. They established a tradition of sharing their knowledge, contacts, marketing know-how, and experiences with newcomers, who in turn shared the same with those who would follow."

Cataclysmic forces of nature set the table for the Walla Walla Valley wine industry, long before any known civilization on the planet had an inkling of making fermented beverages. Sixteen thousand years ago, late Ice Age tsunamis of water escaped a glacier-dammed lake in the western Montana Rockies and washed down the Columbia River basin.

When the so-called Missoula Floods ended, some parts of Eastern Washington were left with areas of rocky topsoils and others were buried deep in deposits of silt and loam. Thousands of years later, each of these various soil types proved vineyard friendly, depending on what varietals winemakers wanted to grow, and whether the vines were planted in sites offering a measure of protection against occasional arctic blasts.

Credit for that discovery went to Walter Clore, a genial Washington State University horticulture professor from a teetotaling Oklahoma family. Landing a job with the college during the Depression, he began to figure out what would grow and where. Over years of research and trials he proved that European wine varietals could survive freezes and thrive in Eastern Washington's microclimates and soils if vineyard sites were chosen with care, and if specific agricultural practices were used.

By the 1970s, as his research bore fruit, Clore had three core believers in the Walla Walla Valley's potential to grow wine grapes—Gary Figgins, a produce cannery machinist of Irish and Italian descent; Rick Small, son of a second-generation wheat farmer; and Baker Ferguson, great-grandson of Baker Boyer Bank founder Dorsey Syng Baker. The wineries they eventually founded—Leonetti Cellar, Woodward Canyon, and L'Ecole N° 41, respectively—became a nucleus that the wider wine world would soon hear about, transforming the town's economy and culture.

WSU horticulturist Dr. Walter Clore.

The founders were bound by a common belief that cooperation trumps competition. They established a tradition of sharing their knowledge, contacts, marketing know-how, and experiences with newcomers, who in turn shared the same with those who would follow.

There was one caveat, however—anyone would be welcomed so long as making quality wines was the top priority. It wasn't out of snobbishness; it was because they knew that with limited areas in Washington where vineyards could survive freezing spells, they could not compete in volume and price against the mass-produced Gallo-type behemoths making roughly 98 percent of the nation's wine in California.

Early on, Washington wines were primarily sweet, high-alcohol generic concoctions, unlike the finer varietal wines of Europe. But Walter Clore believed that the state could be more competitive and profitable by producing European-style wines. The challenge: Where could grape varietals be planted and thrive in Eastern Washington to make quality wines rivaling those of Europe and the exclusive Napa Valley?

Wine grape vines lie dormant during a Walla Walla Valley winter.

Clore began growing vine stock from Europe and California, and over the years he kept detailed notes on his grapes, recording effects of weather, fertilizers, irrigation, ground covers, and different trellising and pruning methods. In the 1960s, he began field trials around Eastern Washington to test the viability of his vines, showing growers they could harvest quality wine grapes using his practices.

The growers got the message: there was a much bigger world in which they could compete. By the end of the decade, growers had planted considerable acreage with certified vinifera vine stock. Not long after that, Clore recalled in a 2002 interview for *Wine Spectator* magazine, "hippies and businessmen and CEOs were all getting into the wine business."

L'Ecole Nº 41 founders Jean and Baker Ferguson.

Testing the Temperatures

The region's growers, vintners, and hobbyists making wine at home often sought advice from Clore and his winemaking research counterparts at WSU, Charles Nagel and George Carter. The three were also often invited to share their knowledge at informal wine-tasting gatherings. Frequently attending these gatherings were Baker and Jean Ferguson, Gary and Nancy Figgins, Rick and Darcey Fugman-Small—at the time also still home winemakers—as well as growers and vintners from the Tri-Cities and Yakima Valley.

Baker Ferguson, then Baker Boyer Bank's president, and Jean would occasionally host those gatherings at their Walla Walla home. A Whitman College economics professor before joining the family bank, he was a well-traveled oenophile who collected fine wines for his

Baker and Jean Ferguson work in their winery during a harvest crush in the early days of L'Ecole Nº 41. Founded in 1983, with Jean as the winemaker, L'Ecole Nº 41 was the third commercial winery in the Walla Walla Valley.

cellar and made his own. His daughter, Megan Clubb, recalled that he would serve some of his purchased cellar wines at gatherings and say, "This is the goal!"

Her father was so devoted to his avocation that when it came time to make wine at home with her parents, it was all hands on deck—like it or not. "I had a final in my sophomore year at high school in 1972 that I needed to study for, and they needed to have the grapes stomped," she said. "So there was this vat and they had me stomping away at the grapes. The test was in the early afternoon, and all morning long I was stomping and my mother was holding a book that I was reading and flipping pages to try to be ready for this test.

"I think what my father brought to the table was a great understanding," she said. "He'd done a lot of studying about Old World wines, and his target was to be competitive with those wines. And as an educator, he had a plan for what he thought could happen."

As a banker, Ferguson practiced due diligence and risk avoidance as a matter of course. He turned that skill to his quest of locating the best vineyard sites in the Walla Walla Valley. As he got to know Clore, Ferguson discovered that successful sites in Eastern Washington had long daily sun exposure and were sloped enough to shed freezing air as it rushed downhill like water, pulling warmer air above it down along the slopes. In vineyards too flat, or in the valley's lower elevations, the colder air pooled into freezing pockets that threatened buds and the cane they grew on. Such killer freezes historically happen in the valley an average of every six years. Indeed, early Italian immigrants who planted American grape vineyards on the valley floor endured enough "Black Frosts" that by 1955, the lone surviving grower, Bert Pesciallo, gave up hope of ever making a business of producing wine in the area.

Armed with thermometers and a record book, Ferguson began tromping over the hills and lowlands to set up temperature-monitoring sites. What he found were sweet spots on hillsides at 1,000 to 1,500 feet in elevation that were several degrees warmer in winter than on the valley floor. That was enough variance to make a difference in whether a grape grower could have a good harvest after a freeze or little to nothing at all.

"He was super excited," Clubb remembered. "I think he would have been terribly disappointed had it not been proven that you could grow wine grapes in the Walla Walla Valley."

Bring On the Vines

Although Ferguson did much to give birth to the valley's modern wine industry, he held off on his dream to start his own winery until a decade later, after he retired as Baker Boyer Bank's president in 1982. He and his wife opened L'Ecole Nº 41 in a three-story 1915 schoolhouse converted to a winery in Lowden, a few miles west of Walla Walla, and next door to the Smalls' Woodward Canyon Winery. Woodward Canyon had opened in 1981 as the valley's second winery.

Painting of the 1915 schoolhouse that was transformed into L'Ecole N° 41's winery and tasting room, in Lowden, west of Walla Walla.

The first winery, the Figgins' Leonetti Cellar, opened in 1977 on the east edge of Walla Walla. Its name honors Figgins' maternal grandparents, Francesco and Rosa Leonetti. They immigrated to the United States from Italy and homesteaded a small farm in Walla Walla in 1906. On an acre and a half of that property's sloped ground, Gary Figgins planted his first commercial vineyard in 1974.

Figgins, and a steady trickle of new vintners starting wineries in the Walla Walla Valley, continued to depend on established growers along the Columbia River and in the Yakima Valley for their grapes. But traveling to monitor contracted grapes in the growing season and then hauling grapes from 50 to 150 miles away was time-consuming and expensive for these small wineries. And ultimately, the product wouldn't truly be considered a Walla Walla wine reflective of the valley's terroir if the key ingredient came from somewhere else.

That dependence began to change in 1980 when Drs. Herbert Hendricks and James McClellan planted their 20-acre Seven Hills Vineyard, which overlooked the valley from its southern hills near Milton-Freewater.

A few years later Norm McKibben, known locally as "Stormin' Norman" for the energy and entrepreneurship he brought to projects, came to the valley. He was a civil engineer by profession who had worked in the Tri-Cities in the early 1980s and retired after developing oil shale fields in Colorado. He and his wife, Virginia, moved to the Walla Walla Valley in 1985. But he wasn't done working. He became acquainted with Mike Hogue, who cofounded The Hogue Cellars in Prosser in 1982. "He got me interested in wine, and I got interested in grapes," McKibben said.

He partnered with a local group of farmers and businessmen who planted a 44-acre vineyard on Canoe Ridge above the Columbia River starting in 1989. He then turned his energy to the Walla Walla Valley, planting his 20-acre Pepper Bridge Vineyard in 1991 near to where, seven years later, he would start his own Pepper Bridge Winery. In 1994, he bought the 20-acre Seven Hills Vineyard. And in 1997, McKibben, partnering with the Figgins, Clubbs, and Bob Rupar, who had helped start Nelson Irrigation Corporation in 1973, bought 150 acres of wheatland east of the adjacent site, and planted Seven Hills East vineyard. In 2001, McKibben built his Les Collines Vineyard on a gentle slope a few miles southeast of Walla Walla in the Blue Mountain foothills. The "retired" engineer introduced state-of-the-art technology in each vineyard, from water-conserving irrigation systems

Gary and Nancy Figgins in front of their original winery in 1979 on their home property in Walla Walla.

to soil moisture and temperature monitoring equipment. All were managed with salmon-safe sustainable farming techniques. Indeed, the advancements produced such high quality that each row in every vineyard was under contract with top premium winemakers in Walla Walla and elsewhere in the state.

But McKibben's biggest project was yet to come and remains under development today: SeVein Vineyards. In 2004, McKibben again partnered with the Figgins, Clubb, and Rupar families and bought 2,700 acres of former wheatland surrounding the Seven Hills complex. About 1,500 acres were available to develop into vineyards by winemakers who purchased 40-acre-minimum lots, water rights included. As of 2018, a total of 1,000 acres had been sold.

STARTING UP, BREAKING OUT

Gary Figgins was confident he could make a decent bottle to sell. He'd made wines with his uncles for home consumption, educated himself on Old World techniques, and joined tastings with other "movers and shakers" in the state's nascent wine industry for years. But just how decent? He was soon to find out with his first vintage in 1978. It included 250 cases of white wines—riesling and gewürztraminer—and 100 cases of cabernet sauvignon made with his own few grapes and others he'd bought from Sagemoor Vineyards near Pasco.

"From the get-go, the very first red wine we made, it was like, Wow!" he said. "They were as good or better than

Left: Gary Figgins unloads rootstock in 1974 for the first planting of the family's Leonetti vineyard.
Right: Figgins' uncles, George and Bill, help plant the vineyard.

Pepper Bridge Winery founder Norm McKibben and winemaker Jean-François Pellet with the arrival of their first wine, a 1998 cabernet sauvignon, in August 2000.

Aerial view of the SeVein Vineyards complex sprawling on hills on the south side of the Walla Walla Valley, 2016.

anything I'd tasted from anywhere else, made with grapes from here and 50 miles around."

But it took a little stardust falling on him in 1981 to help get that message out. With three years of aging, he released his 1978 cab for $15 a bottle. After it received good reviews in a wine competition in the Tri-Cities, he entered a few bottles in a national tasting conducted by *Wine & Spirits* in Atlanta, Georgia. To his amazement still, 38 years later, the judges ranked it the best cabernet sauvignon in America that year.

"It took the whole thing," said Figgins. "That launched us. Can you imagine? Who wouldn't want something like that as a young, upstart winery trying to get attention for quality, and bang, you hit it big."

He eventually ditched his white wines to focus solely on cabernet sauvignon, merlot, and sangiovese, limiting his volume to about 6,800 cases. The wines are so cultishly clamored for that there's a long waiting list to join their wine club and secure access.

Rick Small, a 1969 Washington State University graduate, became interested in wine through his friendship with Figgins that began when they were Army Reserve drill sergeants. Small bought books to learn about winemaking and viticulture and began making his own wines in 1976 with grapes from Figgins' vineyard. He planted his first grapes, chardonnay, on a small plot of dryland wheat field his father let him have to experiment with near the family home. "I think he just wanted me to stay on the farm," Small said, adding that if not for wine he probably would have left agriculture and pursued his interest in architecture.

By 1980, his homemade wines, made with his own grapes and others he'd bought from Columbia Basin growers, were showing well at tastings. Well enough that he and Darcey decided to start their commercial winery in 1981 with financing received through Baker Boyer.

He burnished his reputation as a master of making quality wines that aged well with the release of his sixth vintage. In 1990, *Wine Spectator* magazine ranked his 1987 Dedication Series Cabernet Sauvignon among the top 10 wines not just in America, but in the world. It was the first time a Washington wine hit that exalted level on the prestigious magazine's annual list. Other reds in the top 10 were from France, Italy, and Napa, California, plus a German riesling. "Incredibly fruity, very rich,

Gary Figgins and friend Cliff Kontos crush grapes the old-fashioned way while enjoying a glass of wine in 1975.

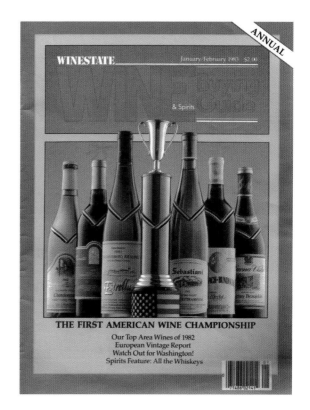

The Figgins' first vintage, a 1978 Leonetti Cellar cabernet sauvignon, won accolades as the best cabernet in America in a national competition in Atlanta, Georgia, in 1982. The February 1983 cover of Wine & Spirits proclaimed, "Watch out for Washington!"

supple, smooth and elegant," *Wine Spectator* described the Woodward Canyon wine. "One of the greatest Washington Cabs we've tasted." It retailed for $19 a bottle, while other cabs on the list ranged from $30 to $240.

L'Ecole N° 41 had some regional success under the Fergusons with its lineup of merlot, semillon, and chenin blanc. But it would really take off after their son-in-law, Marty Clubb, came aboard in the late 1980s. Under his management, L'Ecole gained a national reputation as a top winery, known for consistent year-to-year quality for its many premium varietals.

Marty and Megan Clubb had met in 1980 when both were finance majors in the master's program at MIT's Sloan School of Management in Boston. She had graduated Phi Beta Kappa from Whitman College; he had a chemical engineering degree from Texas A&M.

Marty said his first exposure to fine wines came when Baker Ferguson would visit them in Boston and take them to dinner and order wines from top makers in France and California. "It was a real eye-opening experience," he said. "I'd gone to school in Texas, you know—we drank beer."

After the Clubbs graduated from MIT and married in 1982, they landed jobs with major corporations in San Francisco. When they weren't on business trips, they spent many weekends in the nearby Napa and Sonoma wine country. Marty also took viticulture and enology extension courses through the University of California, Davis. Visits to Walla Walla were usually timed for L'Ecole harvests so they could help get grapes crushed, fermented, and into barrels. Then came the births of their two children—first Riley, then Rebecca—and thoughts of returning to Walla Walla permanently.

"By 1988, the chaos of working 70- to 80-hour weeks, both of us living on airplanes, two kids at home, and challenging support in an expensive environment" was taking a toll, he said. Coincidentally, the Fergusons had been thinking of selling the winery and moving to California to start a vineyard. "This was all just talk, then Megan had the idea of maybe we should move to Walla Walla and get involved in the winery. To be honest, with my background in chemical engineering I was intrigued with fermentation science."

Rick Small punches down a cap of grapes in a fermentation tank during a harvest crush in the early days of Woodward Canyon Winery in Lowden, west of Walla Walla.

Rick Small on the cover of Wine Spectator *magazine in 1992. The prestigious magazine named Small's 1987 Dedication Series Cabernet Sauvignon among the top 10 wines in the world in 1990.*

Among the first things he did when Baker Ferguson handed him the keys to the winery was add cabernet sauvignon to its offerings and increase overall production from 1,000 cases a year to 2,500. "The reason was, we needed to sell more wine to make the thing work," Clubb said. Since then, production, including new varietals and blends added to the lineup, has grown to 45,000 cases.

"Baker was amazingly brilliant. He was intuitively creative. He was the mentor. He envisioned things that were just incredible—but the practical side of execution was really not his forte," Clubb said. "In many respects, what I did when I eventually got here was just executing on his great ideas. For Baker, this was more about creating a fine bottle of wine than it was creating a sound business. I, of course, wanted to do both."

He also got busy establishing relationships with top vineyards in the region and further honing his wine making. It began paying off with medals in enological tastings and regional competitions. In 2001, L'Ecole was heralded nationally when *Wine & Spirits* magazine included it in its annual Top 100 Wineries list. It remained there for 14 consecutive years.

In 2014, the London-based *Decanter* magazine awarded L'Ecole's 2011 Estate Ferguson its International Trophy for best Bordeaux blend in the world. The grapes were from the first crop he harvested from his 40-acre plot, Ferguson Vineyard, at the highest elevation in the SeVein complex.

"That was the biggest coup we've ever had," Clubb said of the *Decanter* competition. Some 60 accredited masters of wine and 20 master sommeliers judged 16,000 entries of various varietals and blends from around the world. "The award—particularly in building our international audience—is the kind of accolade that we'll use forever."

Top: Marty and Megan Clubb stir fermenting juice in a tank at L'Ecole N° 41 during a harvest in the 1980s.

Bottom: Marty Clubb and the premier international wine merchant and critic Steven Spurrier at the 2014 Decanter awards in London, England.

Baker Boyer's 150th blend goes through the bottling and labeling line at L'Ecole N° 41 in 2019.

BUILDING A WINE JUGGERNAUT

The widely publicized successes of Leonetti Cellar, Woodward Canyon, and L'Ecole served as a magnet to others wanting to get in on the action in Walla Walla. It started as a trickle, with 10 producing wineries in 1998. By 2003, it had become a torrent, with 45 producers with wines on the market, and a tripling of that by 2018.

They've come from all walks—young vintners from Europe and California seeking to establish their own reputations for style and quality; people from around the country beginning their careers; people investing their equity into second or third careers. Well-to-do people making their mark and money in sports, entertainment, and technology and wanting to live the wine lifestyle also joined the ranks.

Marty Clubb attributed the increase in the pace of growth after 1998 to two things that started up around 2000, and ultimately "became the toolbox for the wine industry in Walla Walla."

The first was the formation of the Walla Walla Valley Wine Alliance. It was composed of vintners and growers seeking to ensure that quality remained foremost in the local industry by using best practices for winemaking and employing sustainable, environmentally friendly agriculture methods in the vineyards. The Alliance's assistance was available to anyone who sought it. It also served as a marketing arm for the valley, a kind of chamber of commerce for wine that could promote the valley in the media, organize tasting events, and put wineries in touch with retailers and distributors, and vice versa.

The Walla Walla valley wineries put out their first wine-tasting map in 1996, showing locations of the Valley's eight wineries.

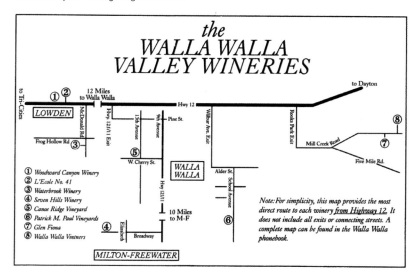

Corey Braunel (left) and Chad Johnson (far right), two of Dusted Valley's owners, at their wine production facility with Baker Boyer's Elizabeth Humphrey, VP and Business Advisor (middle left), and Susie Colombo, VP and Family Advisor (middle right).

PARTNERING WITH WINERIES

BAKER BOYER WAS an early partner with many of the first wineries and vineyards. This partnership proves that a community working together can be a powerful force—verified by the numerous worldwide awards local wines have received.

Rick Small recalled working with Baker Boyer in the early 1980s when he and his wife, Darcey Fugman-Small, began Woodward Canyon. The award-winning winery was named for the canyon where Small's family farmed for multiple generations. "I was probably their first wine client," said Small. "That's the thing about Baker Boyer over the years—you talk about them as if they are lenders, but they're really partners. We've kind of grown together. And I've been fortunate enough to work with some pretty good loan officers."

Russ Colombo, senior vice president and senior business advisor, has worked with wineries since the early '90s. "What I enjoy most is the passion they have in what they are doing," said Colombo. "Over the years, I have also enjoyed my clients' vision and subsequent teaming with other wineries and winemakers to make Walla Walla a renowned wine region by creating some of the best wines in the world!"

Helping clients succeed is the bottom line for Elizabeth Humphrey, vice president and business advisor, who works with many wineries. "Wineries are quite different from other types of businesses," said Humphrey. "Wine is one of the most challenging industries out there." She advises new clients to surround themselves with industry-experienced mentors, including their banker, CPA, and attorney, who understand wine inventory, pricing, and cash-flow issues unique to the industry.

"Winery owners pour their heart, soul, and personal finances into the winery during the first several years of operations to keep it going," said Humphrey. "As a lender, my greatest days are when I get to see that winery turn the corner and become a successful, cash-flow business operation that the owners are proud of and that can sustain them for years to come."

Darcey Fugman-Small and Clubb were key players in getting the membership organization started. "We kind of led the effort to create it and it happened in 2000, then really got off the ground in 2001," said Clubb, who served as president of the Alliance from inception to 2006. "All the wineries joined in."

The second thing, Clubb said, was the creation of the Center for Enology and Viticulture at Walla Walla Community College in 2000. The idea for it was pushed by the college's president, Steve VanAusdle, widely respected for creating innovative career programs tailored to various regional industries that were looking for trained employees. Myles Anderson, the college's director of counseling, became the center's director. He and winemaker friend Gordy Venneri had established the valley's eighth winery, Walla Walla Vintners, in 1995.

The two-year program got underway in 2000, the first of its kind in the nation offered at a community college. Hands-on training was provided at local vineyards and wineries while plans were laid for the new center. Classes—from viticulture, to the science of making wine, to the art of marketing it—were taught on campus. Word about the program spread regionally and then nationally, with students young and older wanting to enroll.

"It just went crazy," VanAusdle said in a 2003 interview when the center's $4.1 million building on campus opened. "It spilled over into something much bigger than we ever thought."

With a teaching vineyard of many varietals planted nearby, the building has classrooms and a full-scale winery where students make College Cellars brand wines. The wines are sold at the center to help fund the program and frequently medal in professional competitions. The center later added a professional kitchen when a culinary program was developed.

Top: Students work the first crush at Walla Walla Community College's new Center for Enology and Viticulture, the nation's first working winery operated at a community college.

Bottom: Students in WWCC's wine program receive hands-on vineyard experience.

Bottling the Baker Boyer anniversary blend at L'Ecole, 2019.

BAKER BOYER'S 150TH BLEND

SPECIAL OCCASIONS CALL for special wines. For the 150th anniversary of Baker Boyer Bank, the oldest bank in the state, L'Ecole N° 41 winery created a red blend made with grapes from one of the oldest and most highly acclaimed vineyards in the Walla Walla Valley.

The Baker Boyer 2017 Mélange D'Héritage, French for "Legacy Blend," is made of merlot, cabernet sauvignon, and cabernet franc grapes from Seven Hills Vineyard, first planted in 1980, and a source of L'Ecole's many award-winning wines since 1993.

Forty-eight cases were made to celebrate the bank's milestone birthday, November 10, 2019, and to toast the vitality of the region and the generous spirit of the people who make the Valley a special place

Clubb credited VanAusdle for his "incredible vision, like many of the great visions he had, to build the center." The establishment of the center and other regional industry programs was a key factor a decade later when the Aspen Institute ranked the school the best community college in the nation. "Churning out 30 to 35 students every year for 18 years has translated into a very large influence on Washington's wine industry," Clubb said. "Of the collective number of 90-plus-scoring wines in Washington, half of those were made by students who graduated from the center. They're everywhere. It's pretty amazing."

Numbers also drive the narrative in the continuing story of wine in the Walla Walla Valley and in Washington overall.

From the few acres Figgins and Small had planted before their first vintages, by 2018 the valley had 3,000 acres of French, Italian, Spanish, and German wine grapes, grown by more than 25 vineyard operations, with more acres to be planted. Statewide vineyard acreage in 2018 had topped 55,000, with 350 growers. Red wine grapes led with 64 percent of production.

As for wineries, the number in the Walla Walla Valley had grown from three producers in 1983 to more than 120 in 2018, with more in startup stages. Statewide, 940 were operating in 2018, producing nearly 17.5 million cases. Washington's wine commission reported that the industry had a $4.8 billion total impact on the state's economy that year.

Walter Clore's notion that Washington could compete with the world in producing premium-quality wines had become fact. His efforts were recognized by the Legislature in 2001, when at age 90 and still helping growers choose vineyard sites and what to plant, he was officially declared the "Father of Washington's Wine Industry."

"His impact was huge," Yakima Valley winemaker Mike Sauer said in a 2002 interview. With Clore's guidance, Sauer planted his acclaimed Red Willow Vineyard in the 1970s. "As one of nature's gentlemen, he's always shown kindness to whoever is seeking information about growing wine grapes," he said of Clore. "He took me seriously, perhaps more seriously than I took myself." Clore died in 2003 at his home in Prosser.

The same could be said about Clore's friend in the Walla Walla Valley, Baker Ferguson, who died in 2005. Both were visionaries who had the warmth and collaborative people skills to make things happen. Their goals were not just for themselves but also, in their hearts and well-educated minds, for the state and for the welcoming, picturesque valley in Washington's southeast corner.

Picking crew works a harvest in SeVein Vineyards.

A flotilla of hot-air balloons float over Walla Walla during the 2015 Walla Walla Balloon Stampede, an annual event initiated in 1974.

CHAPTER 6

Securing the Future of Community

"Without locally-owned businesses, there is no 'Main Street,' and without local business leaders, there is no Main Street revitalization."

— 2002 National Main Street Center Award citation

Downtown Walla Walla had arrived at a new business and development plateau by 1920. Main Street and blocks north and south were a honeycomb of commerce and retail serving the city's 15,500 residents and the greater population beyond.

Dirt streets were paved, lighted, and lined with sidewalks. The wood buildings of its pioneer days had been replaced with brick and masonry edifices, with the Baker Boyer Bank building, completed in 1911, the tallest at seven stories.

But amid the growth, the town's infrastructure still lacked something that Spokane, Seattle, Boise, Portland, and other regional commercial hub cities in the Pacific Northwest already had: a first-class, landmark hotel. Such a destination hotel that would attract visitors, business travelers, and conventions had been discussed for years in Walla Walla as a way to distinguish the town and fuel further

Construction of the Marcus Whitman Hotel in 1928. Completed in September of that year, the landmark building still remained the tallest structure in Walla Walla in 2019.

economic growth. But it took an announcement in 1927 by W.W. Baker, the fourth president of Baker Boyer Bank, to set things in motion for the construction of The Marcus Whitman Hotel.

He had been in touch with a Seattle development firm, Real Estate Improvement Company, which had inquired about building a multistory hotel in Walla Walla. The company proposed to invest $300,000 toward building it if the town could come up with another $150,000 in 90 days. Baker was intrigued and wrote a letter to the Chamber of Commerce to invite members to a meeting so he could introduce the proposal. More than 200 members showed up, an indicator of the depth and breadth of Walla Walla's committed business community at the time.

"If this proposal is accepted, a high grade hotel will be secured at a very slight cost," Baker was quoted as telling the Chamber audience in a history of the city written by Robert Bennett in the early 1980s. "I do not believe that an opportunity with as favorable conditions will come to us again."

The proposal was enthusiastically accepted in an oft-repeated example of the town rallying behind innovative entrepreneurial ideas to further the community's long-term interests. A committee was formed to manage the sale of stock in the development company. It was headed by Baker, his son-in-law Craig Ferguson, and hardware store owner Oscar Drumheller. Selling for $100 per share, the committee secured the $150,000 in local funding—equivalent to raising $2.2 million in 2018 dollars—in a little more than a month. J.L. "Jerry" Cundiff, who worked at, and would later own, Falkenbergs Jewelers, was credited as the committee member who sold the most shares.

With a design by architect Sherwood D. Ford, construction of the 173-room hotel at Rose Street and Second Avenue began in September 1927. The grand opening was held on September 6, 1928, with W.W. Baker given the honor of being the first to sign The Marcus Whitman's guest register.

At 12 stories, the hotel remains the tallest building in Walla Walla. It was one of few in the country to have its lobby, ballroom, and guest rooms crafted by an interior designer, and one of the first in the West to incorporate heating and air conditioning in a single system throughout the hotel.

It was an immediate hit, accommodating guests in 113 rooms in its first two days of operation and booking the 1928 annual meeting of the Washington Good Roads Association later that year, according to the *Walla Walla Union*. "And many more gatherings of importance are expected also to be won largely through assurance that hereafter Walla Walla can care for the largest of conventions likely to be available."

Among noted guests during its glory days from the late 1920s to early 1960s were entertainers Louis Armstrong and Shirley Temple and television actors George Reeves (*Adventures of Superman*) and Chuck Connors (*The Rifleman*). President Dwight D. Eisenhower stayed at the hotel in 1954 during a visit to the region to dedicate McNary Dam, and Vice President Lyndon Johnson, here to dedicate the Ice Harbor Dam, was a guest in 1962.

"MOVERS AND SHAKERS"

With a grand hotel now part of Walla Walla's infrastructure, folks had a place to stay and do business in the growing city, but it still

Left: Francis Stiller, a member of the Walla Walla Wagon Wheelers, astride a horse in the Whitman Hotel in May 1962. The club represents the Walla Walla Valley in area celebrations, using horses, wagons, and western dress.

Right: Edward M. "Ted" Kennedy campaigns at the Marcus Whitman Hotel on August 25, 1960, for his brother, U.S. presidential candidate Sen. John F. Kennedy, who went on to become America's 35th president.

needed to connect more easily to the larger world. The rapid rise of commercial aviation became the obvious answer. Establishing commercial air service to Walla Walla would be no small feat. First of all, the current small airstrip was not nearly the size it needed to be to accommodate larger aircraft. Again, it was the business community in collaboration with the city and voters that made it happen.

The first Walla Walla air derby was held in May 1928 at the new airstrip. The event helped fuel interest in the economic potential of aviation, and a municipal airport association was incorporated. The following spring the association and the Chamber of Commerce began a project to build a larger airport. J.L. Cundiff, the jeweler noted for his local fundraising prowess for The Marcus Whitman, took charge of a $50,000 successful bond election in 1929, to buy a portion of what grew into the present-day Walla Walla Regional Airport. Cundiff was named the first chairman of the airport board when the city took over the airport in 1930—it eventually relinquished ownership to the Port of Walla Walla in 1989.

Cundiff, born in Arkansas a younger son in a poor family that moved to Walla Walla to start a wheat farm, had a drive and sense of community spirit and purpose that could rally others to a good cause. Such traits are not uncommon among people who've made a difference in the town before and since. Cundiff's dedication, carried

Walla Walla's thriving Main Street, circa 1920. Much of the architectural detail on buildings was covered under façades of stucco, sheet metal, and large signs in ensuing years. A 1990s downtown restoration project returned the street close to its original look.

on by his son's and grandson's community efforts, serves as a microcosm of the multigenerational spirit that has kept the city moving forward.

"He was always just one who got involved with business leaders," said his grandson, J.L. "Skip" Cundiff, the third generation of the family to own and operate Falkenbergs Jewelers on Main Street, with its historic 1906 mechanical clock on a stand outside the store that still keeps time with weekly wind-ups. "He was a mover and shaker in his day, and where that drive came from I don't know. He came from a pretty meager farm family."

In 1914, while still in high school, J.L. Cundiff started working as a bookkeeper in the shop Kristian Falkenberg established in the Die Brücke Building in 1906. "In those days the older sons continued farming and the younger sons, if the farm's not big enough, had to go in different directions," Skip Cundiff said.

In 1932, J.L. Cundiff and watchmaker Knute Glimme formed a partnership and bought the store from Falkenberg. When Glimme died in the 1960s, Cundiff and his son, Jerry "Spud" Cundiff Jr., became partners in the store. The Cundiff family legacy continued when Skip Cundiff began working at the store in 1975 with his father after graduating from Walla Walla Community College. Skip is now the owner.

The "mover and shaker" gene of his grandfather apparently was passed down, with all three generations of Cundiffs having served on Chamber of Commerce boards and in several community service clubs. His son, Jesse, the fourth generation, started working at Falkenbergs in 2013.

To all four generations, Skip Cundiff said, the jewelry store's allure is that "you get to help people celebrate the milestones in their lives—getting engaged, anniversaries, birthdays. People are usually coming in here to celebrate something, and it's a nice business to be in from that standpoint."

But with his decades-long view outside the store's front window, Cundiff saw increasingly less to celebrate in the downtown district as it entered a downward slide from the 1970s through the early 1990s. The slide was by all accounts a major crisis for a community. It was due

The 1928 Walla Walla Air Derby was held at a small airstrip. The event fueled interest among local leaders to build a municipal airport to handle more and larger aircraft.

Street scene looking west from First Avenue and Main Street, circa 1934.

to a combination of factors, starting with the Middle East oil shocks in the 1970s that triggered rampant inflation and soaring interest rates in the United States, crimping consumers' wallets and making borrowing expensive. Then, several major retailers left downtown as shopping malls sprang up on the outskirts of Walla Walla and in the Tri-Cities in the 1980s. The Marcus Whitman, too, suffered under a series of owners that let it degrade to a point where visitors stopped staying there. Half-hearted attempts to turn it into condos and low-rent apartments were no help, with owners doing little to maintain sanitation and building upkeep.

"There wasn't a lot left," Cundiff recalled. "There weren't any restaurants and there wasn't a lot of reason for people to come downtown. People always thought Walla Walla was a great place to raise a family, but once you go on there's not a lot of reason to come back because there wasn't much here."

There was, however, a lot of never-say-die in the community. This spirit fueled a major collaborative push by building owners, merchants, entrepreneurs, and city officials to resurrect the downtown district and usher in a new era of "glory days." Too, there were a growing number of high-quality premium wineries that attracted attention to the community in wine, food, and lifestyle media and served as a springboard to increasing tourism. But first, the downtown needed a serious facelift to give tourists something to see and do in the historical town when they weren't visiting wineries.

Back to the Future

Although the retail flight pushed the vacancy rate in downtown commercial buildings to 30 percent in the mid-1980s, there was still a major jewel in the crown, The Bon Marché (since rebranded as Macy's after acquisition by parent company Federated Department Stores). Walla Walla native Libby Frazier was The Bon's general manager who, Cundiff said, "fought hard to keep it downtown." She was a local

Top: The Liberty Theatre, built in 1917 with Dutch-style architectural influences, in its heyday.

Bottom: The theater as it appeared in its faded glory on Main Street in 1987 prior to renovation.

Cyclists race past the Liberty Theatre building as it looks today. The Bon Marché, now Macy's, expanded into the former theater in a major renovation in 1991. That renovation led the way in an effort to restore downtown buildings to their original luster.

The Reynolds-Day Building at the start of the renovation as crews prepare to remove the sheet metal façade in 1993.

businesswoman who believed Main Street's historic buildings held the seeds of a renaissance.

The Bon was located at the corner of Main and Colville Streets, next door to the classic, three-story Dutch-style Liberty Theatre. The 1917 building was unique among theaters, with its white glazed terra cotta with blue accents, red tile roof, and two dormers on a steeply pitched roof. It had closed in the early 1980s when multiplex cinemas came to town. With Frazier's urging and recruiting of city support, The Bon in January 1991 announced a $650,000 plan to restore the theater's exterior and renovate the interior to expand the store into it. City Manager Harry Kinzer worked with local banks to loan $200,000. The *Walla Walla Union-Bulletin* reported that another $200,000 of federal money channeled through the city was available for the project. Work began in March 1991 and was completed by mid-August.

Robert Mang, former president of The Bon, credited local customer loyalty and Frazier for making the Liberty Theatre project possible. "Libby Frazier has literally driven Bon executives to distraction on the project," he was quoted in the newspaper. "It shows what can be done on sheer determination."

The next year the city completed a $2.2 million Main Street revival project that included widened sidewalks, added brickwork, turn-of-the-century lighting, a small park, street-side tree plantings, and other amenities. The new streetscape and the Liberty Theatre project set an example of what could be done with blocks of Main Street buildings whose original brick exteriors were hidden behind

The Reynolds-Day Building as it looks after being restored to its original 1874 exterior. The first constitutional convention of Washington Territory was held on the upper floor of this building in the summer of 1878.

façades of stucco, sheet metal, and mid-1900s signage clutter. "Some of the property owners decided to take a little more pride in their property from the example of the Liberty Theatre," Cundiff said. They had help available through the Downtown Walla Walla Foundation, a nonprofit group formed in the mid-1980s to improve and promote the city's central commercial district. It helped owners of historic buildings secure state funds for preservation projects and manage work contracts.

It was a service that Skip Cundiff and his father, who had moved Falkenbergs Jewelers a block west on Main Street in 1974 when he bought the 100-year-old Reynolds-Day Building, were grateful for when they decided in 1993 to renovate it. Their building had a matchless pedigree: The state's first constitutional convention was held upstairs on the second floor in 1878. The Cundiffs removed the metal façade on the exterior and returned its brick and masonry to its original luster. The project cost about $200,000, Skip Cundiff said, with $75,000 of that from a state historic preservation grant. It was the second renovation project after the Liberty Theatre, and soon other commercial property owners and merchants jumped on the bandwagon with more projects through the end of the decade.

But downtown's crown jewel, The Marcus Whitman, remained in disrepair until 1999, when it was bought by Kyle Mussman, an independently wealthy entrepreneur from the Midwest. He came to Walla Walla in 1989 to establish a regional cellular phone business, he said. In buying the hotel, he envisioned a $35 million renovation and expansion project. The renovation would include luxury suites and deluxe rooms, high-speed internet connections, a first-class restaurant—The Marc—with a focus on local wines, and a convention center with 10,000 square feet of conference space to hold events for 100 to 400 people.

"I wanted to give the community something we all could be proud of," he said. "I had been driving past the hotel for 10 years, watching it disintegrate. Here's this grand old building, part of the heartbeat of Walla Walla at one time, and half of downtown was boarded up."

The project was partially financed with a total $9 million consortium loan from Baker Boyer Bank, Bank of the West, and Banner Bank. Megan Clubb recalled why Baker Boyer chose to step up to the

Southwestward view of the Marcus Whitman Hotel before its renovation began in 1999.

plate for the renovation. "It had to do with reinvesting in the community and reestablishing The Marcus Whitman as a vital community asset," she said.

Mussman hired Portland-based Fletcher Farr Ayotte, now known as FFA Architecture and Interiors, to design the renovation because of its experience in rehabilitating historic buildings. Specialists with the firm found the hotel's original building plans at the University of Washington archives, photos from the *Walla Walla Union* showing what the interior looked like at its grand opening, and ads from manufacturers showing some of the lobby and room furnishings they sold to the hotel.

The goal was to replicate the original design while adding modern safety features including seismically upgraded walls, new mechanical and electrical systems, fire alarms, and sprinkler systems. All of it had to be invisible to maintain the building's historic integrity, according to an article FFA published about the renovation. After 14 months of construction, the renovated and renamed Marcus Whitman Hotel & Conference Center opened in 2001.

"We got tremendous support and cooperation from the City of Walla Walla," FFA project manager Phil Rude said in the article. "They really embraced this project, which helped the process flow very well. But it was Kyle who had the vision for the project as being of the highest quality. He was really willing to go the extra mile to make the Marcus Whitman a truly memorable place."

A decade of revitalizing downtown construction had come to an end, undoing two decades of decline. And with downtown in 2001 looking more like it did in 1901, the National Trust for Historic Preservation bestowed its Great American Main Street Award on Walla Walla. National and regional travel, leisure, and lifestyle magazines soon followed suit, including Walla Walla on various "best" lists. With more tourists coming in for both the historical and wine ambiance, new restaurants opened, offering cuisines other than convenient or home-style Americana. Artists, more live entertainment options, boutique retailers, and new lodging establishments soon followed.

Many locals give the rise of the wine industry the credit for spawning the revitalization of Walla Walla. Rick Small, the founder in 1981 of the highly regarded Woodward Canyon Winery, takes a broader view. "It wasn't just the wine industry, but . . . the downtown development association and the Chamber," he said. "It was a synergy of things beginning to happen that brought diversity and balance downtown. It grew organically. We had these charming, beautiful old classic buildings and we had a story. We still do."

The Marcus Whitman Hotel & Conference Center after its $35 million renovation and expansion in 2001.

BAKER BOYER HONORED NATIONALLY FOR BUSINESS LEADERSHIP

IT TAKES A VILLAGE to help raise a child. But to help raise a village and ensure its economic health and well-being, it takes a committed, community-minded bank.

Baker Boyer was noted for just such a role in revitalizing Walla Walla's historic, but seriously ailing, downtown commercial and retail district in a decade-long renovation effort that culminated in 2001.

That year the National Main Street Center, a subsidiary of the National Trust for Historic Preservation, honored Walla Walla with its Great American Main Street Award for the project. Street work and restoring buildings to their historic grandeur involved collaboration among the city, its Downtown Walla Walla Foundation, commercial building owners and merchants, and the community at large.

In 2002, Baker Boyer was singled out to receive the National Main Street Center's annual Business Leadership award. The citation accompanying the honor stated:

Without locally-owned businesses, there is no "Main Street," and without local business leaders, there is no Main Street revitalization.

Downtown Walla Walla, Washington, has been blessed with the unique local business leadership from Baker Boyer Bank. Operating on the same corner—and run by the same family—for over a century, Baker Boyer Bank has been a driving force in revitalization that led to last year's designation of Walla Walla as a Great American Main Street.

Led today [2002] by the great-great granddaughter of founder D.S. Baker, President and CEO Megan Clubb, Baker Boyer's contributions to downtown revitalization serve as a model for Main Street partnerships. More than thirty historic buildings have been restored with their lending assistance, and last year alone, the bank leveraged its own marketing budget to support the "Shop Downtown" campaign by purchasing and distributing more than $8,000 worth of Downtown Dollars gift certificates.

Yet the bank's most impressive contribution has been in the literally thousands of volunteer hours—from the president to the front tellers—to serve on every committee and promotion for downtown. Under Megan Clubb's stewardship, Baker Boyer continues to set the pace, and earns both local and national distinction for Main Street "Business Leadership" for 2002.

"Future-Proofing"

With Walla Walla's economic story now riding high on tourism and a wine country lifestyle, Baker Boyer President Mark Kajita thinks about what the next chapter will be. Diversifying the economy by building a technology-based sector with companies offering high-paying jobs is where his thoughts lead him.

"As technology continues to evolve—you see it in the banking industry, you're seeing it in the agricultural industry, you're seeing it just everywhere—jobs that are transaction-type or just a single process will be taken over by machines in the future," he said. "So the goal is to future-proof the community. If you are doing that, what you should be doing is trying to bring in technology companies that are actually making the machines and software."

Working with the Port of Walla Walla, Kajita cracked open this door in 2017 by recruiting Ingeniux, a Seattle pioneer in creating highly flexible and secure content management software for publishing websites and other digital content. Its customers include financial services, colleges, and government entities, among others with needs to present constantly changing data and media scalable to desktops, handheld devices, and large screen displays.

Ingeniux was founded in 2000 by Jim Edmunds, a Whitman College graduate who's been involved in the technology industry in Seattle since the early 1990s, and with whom Kajita became associated when he was working at Whitman with high-end donors. "I have always been fascinated by Jim because he was not only a hard worker but also a wise businessman," Kajita said, adding that Ingeniux survived the 2008-2009 recession when a lot of tech companies didn't. "He understood the ebbs and flows of business and how to make them all work out."

Early in Edmunds' career he worked for MSNBC, when it was the largest news website in the world, and where the notion of starting Ingeniux and its innovative decoupled content management system came to him. "I was in charge of the technology platform there," he said. "My colleagues and I had an idea that there was a better way to build this mousetrap, and it had to do with separating the content layer from the presentation layer, so content can be optimized for presentation based on the medium or channel that it is being distributed to."

Mark Kajita with Jim Edmunds, Ingeniux president and CEO, at the Ingeniux office in Walla Walla.

As of 2019, Ingeniux has grown steadily to 60 employees in its Seattle and Walla Walla offices and people located around the world. So, why site an office in Walla Walla when the centers of technology and innovation are in Seattle and the San Francisco Bay Area? As Edmunds replied, it's due to the many things that its residents already know about the welcoming, collaborative, affordable, and sophisticated small town.

"The key to success in the technology industry is having great people, being able to find great people and being able to retain them," Edmunds said. "We are a little bit unique in the industry in that we have an incredible retention rate but we always worry about our company assets walking out the door. There are lots of technology companies that are very successful at finding great people but not very successful at retaining them. That's not our model."

Apart from retention, another factor is the cost of running a business amid the explosion in high-tech development in Seattle, with companies from the Bay Area also setting up operations there. "The cost even to just have office space is going way up, and the cost for people is going way up."

So about five years ago, Edmunds said, Ingeniux started thinking about what to do in the future to continue to be successful in recruiting and retaining new employees with the required technical expertise. The answer was to maintain the company's loyal corps in Seattle and look for a desirable community outside the metropolitan area to expand, hiring locally and letting current employees relocate if they choose. Criteria for such a place, he said, included it being off the West Coast, in a town that had colleges or universities to recruit from, and a quality of life with "very short commute times, great community activities, an inclusive family environment, and culture. Those aren't things that are always easy to find in smaller towns, but there are small towns in America that have that in spades."

Ingeniux CEO Jim Edmunds meets with employees (left to right) Wendy Lennox, Gia Yera, and Efriem Bazabih at the Ingeniux Walla Walla office.

After visits to Spokane; Boise; Des Moines, Iowa; Jackson, Mississippi; and Durham, North Carolina, Ingeniux decided on Walla Walla. A big factor in that choice was Walla Walla Community College. "It's one of the best community colleges in the nation. They are an incredible asset to the community," said Edmunds. "We are really happy with the computer science program and the willingness of their faculty and staff to engage with us to meet our needs." Another factor in choosing Walla Walla was its wine industry. "It's created a culture in Walla Walla that resonates with high-tech industry people we would be recruiting from areas like Seattle and San Francisco," Edmunds said. "We can go to somebody who is working at Google on their Santa Clara campus in the South Bay, San Francisco. They are making a six-figure salary and still the closest house they can afford is a two-hour commute each way. We want to tell them, 'Look, you will take a bit of a pay cut coming to Walla Walla, but we are going to save you four hours a day commuting. You are going to have a beautiful house in a great community with a five-minute drive to work. You have great restaurants, cool coffee shops, over 120 wineries, live music downtown every weekend, and you can go to every single one of your kids' soccer games.'"

A third factor about Walla Walla, Edmunds said, is simply that it's "just a wonderful community. When I bring people over from the Seattle offices . . . the first thing they say is, 'Everything is so clean here.' The second thing they say is, 'Everybody is so friendly here. I walked to coffee and people smiled at me and said hello.' Not what you're going to get in Seattle when you walk down to coffee."

When Ingeniux was thinking about opening an office in Walla Walla, Kajita put Edmunds in touch with the Port of Walla Walla commissioners leading the economic development entity for Walla Walla County. "They were very keen to look for ways to stimulate economic development in the Walla Walla Valley that wasn't service related and that would balance some of the more manufacturing and ag-related business developments they were involved in," Edmunds said. The commissioners put together a business package for the company, found a building in downtown Walla Walla, fixed up its exterior, and created a long-term lease plan. Ingeniux then spent $500,000 to build out the interior to accommodate its office needs. During the construction, Baker Boyer Bank let Ingeniux use its former College Place branch as a temporary operating space for several months, charging it only the cost of utilities.

But no one person or entity, not even the bank, can go it alone. It all boils down to relationships, and coming up with a solution that is really good for the community.

— Mark Kajita

Edmunds said he couldn't be happier about the move. The office opened in October 2017 and now has 17 employees, with space for another 10 before it will need additional office space. Only one of those is a transplant from Seattle—a young married man who pays less for a house in Walla Walla than he did for a small apartment on Capitol Hill in Seattle. Everyone else in Walla Walla has been hired locally. "We could not be happier with the quality of people we're getting from the local community," Edmunds said. He said Ingeniux plans to continue to hire and grow its presence in Walla Walla and "be a very active and positive influence on building a high-tech community in the Walla Walla Valley."

He also singled out Kajita and Baker Boyer Bank for their commitment to the betterment of the community and long-term vision for its economic future. "Mark really got the whole ball rolling," Edmunds said. "The bank has been a great business advisor to us. We quickly switched all of our banking relationships to Baker Boyer. Baker Boyer is like this jewel that a lot of people don't even know exists. . . . It's really a sophisticated investment bank that's wrapped in a very friendly hometown community bank."

Kajita hopes this first step will be a foundation for starting a tech center in Walla Walla. "Baker Boyer has been a great fan of not only entrepreneurship but also of diversifying the economy with good-paying jobs," he said, "and we saw in Ingeniux a great opportunity for us to intervene quickly to bring in a whole new industry." But no one person or entity, not even the bank, can go it alone, he added, noting the Port of Walla Walla and the city's involvement in clearing the way for Ingeniux. "It all boils down to relationships, and coming up with a solution that is really good for the community."

Walla Wallans, especially those who went through the 1970s and 1980s, know that as well. Community is something that requires constant, collaborative building and maintenance. It is, after all, why people come to, stay in, and return to Walla Walla.

The Carnegie Library under construction, circa 1904.

CHAPTER 7

Building Community Culture

NURTURING MINDS AND MUSES

From knowledge comes art, and from art comes knowledge, in a never-ending cycle. The interplay between the two is a hallmark of Walla Walla. The love of learning, literature, music, and the visual arts is woven deeply into the roots of the community's vibrant culture.

For Dorsey Baker, education came first, and his interest in advancing it was piqued by his friend Cushing Eells, a Congregational Church minister. Eells asked if Baker could provide the land for the construction of a new seminary, later to become Whitman College. It would be named in honor of Marcus and Narcissa Whitman.

Baker's three oldest children had been attending a makeshift primary school at the rear of a Main Street store that the fledgling Walla Walla School District No. 1—the first in the territory—had been renting since 1862. The school taught the basic three-Rs—reading, writing, and arithmetic—to the 93 pioneer students who were enrolled by 1864.

Eells described his vision for a seminary for young and older children that would include pre-college courses in higher mathematics and languages. Baker was the beneficiary of a basic education that had carried him through his youth in Illinois to graduating from Jefferson Medical College in Philadelphia, but he wanted a more challenging curriculum for his children. He gave four acres of his home lands to Eells.

Whitman Seminary was built in 1866 on land donated by Dorsey S. Baker. In 1883, the territorial legislature issued a charter changing the seminary into the four-year Whitman College.

Baker School in the 1920s. Built in 1882 on Cherry Street, the public school included primary and high-school-level classes. It was named Baker School in honor of the large donation that Dorsey S. Baker made for its construction.

"Beyond all question this was the choicest of the lands owned by Dr. Baker and is the most desirable residential property in Walla Walla—made so by a stream, bordered by very beautiful native birch, winding its way across the property," wrote W.W. Baker about his father's donation. The parcel was bordered to the north by Boyer Avenue and to the west by Park Street.

In the fall of 1866, Whitman Seminary opened for its first 11-week term. Baker enrolled his three eldest children—Frank, 15, Mary, 13, and Henry, 12—as well as his youngest, five-year-old W.W., then called Willie. In his book, *Forty Years a Pioneer*, W.W. included a tuition receipt his father kept from that first term. Basic classes were $10 per student, with Latin lessons for Frank and Mary an extra five dollars each, for a total of $50.

In her biography of her grandfather Dorsey Baker, Helen Baker Reynolds related stories from her father, Frank Baker, and Uncle Henry about why learning Latin was "essential" to the family patriarch. "Latin means learning," responded her father, who could still diagram the grammatical mechanics of the ancient language in his last years of life. Her uncle told her about how strict his father was about mastering lessons. "Henry recalled in later life that perfect recitation of the day's assignment in Latin and geometry was an absolute requirement before he could have his breakfast."

Whitman Seminary, however, began to falter with declining enrollment as the public school system developed. The town's school had moved from that rented room on Main Street to a wood schoolhouse on Cherry Street in 1866. On the same Cherry Street site in 1882, a large brick building was erected that included primary and high-school-level classes. It was named Baker School in honor of the large donation Dorsey Baker made to build it.

In 1883, the territorial legislature issued a charter changing the seminary into the four-year Whitman College. It offered degrees in liberal arts and sciences.

In 1913, it became the first among the nation's colleges and universities to require comprehensive exams for students in their majors. In 1919, a chapter of Phi Beta Kappa, the oldest and most prestigious academic honors society, was installed. It was the first such chapter for a Pacific Northwest college and underscored Whitman's reputation for excellence. In recent decades it has been perennially ranked among the top private liberal arts colleges in the nation.

Throughout its growth and evolution, generations of the extended Baker family have joined with the community to help ensure success for the college. No fewer than 32 Baker descendants have attended or graduated from Whitman, and 23 have served in faculty, administrative, trustee, and oversight positions. Baker Ferguson, a 1939 graduate, also served on the economics faculty from 1946 to 1948 and later on the board of overseers. Chair of the board of trustees from 1972 to 1983, Ferguson also served on the steering committee for the record-breaking Campaign for Whitman, which raised $52 million for the college. In 2004, the college board of trustees announced that the new $10 million fitness center would be named the Baker Ferguson Fitness Center. "Few people have contributed more to both the success and spirit of Whitman College than Baker Ferguson," said former Whitman President Tom Cronin.

Baker men and women also have donated land for the campus and funds for expansion projects, and willed thousands of acres of family lands to Whitman's endowment fund. Cronin, in speeches to local business groups and alumni during his 1993-2005 tenure, often worked in a play on the phrase "If there's a will there's a way," saying, "If there's a will . . . we want to be in it."

As Whitman benefited, so did Walla Walla. The college's success spilled into the community with the fruits of its music and art departments as well as its graduates who established careers in business and the professions in the valley.

Whitman College's main administration building, Memorial Hall, was constructed in 1899 and remains the oldest building on campus.

Lifelong Learning for All

The symbiotic relationship between community and library has long been apparent in Walla Walla. It got off to an early start in the 1860s when local literary groups, recognizing the need for a library, tried a subscription-based program. It was a noble effort but fell short of being a sustainable library. It would take residents who shared a love of lifelong learning, and a nudge from a Baker daughter and her husband, to secure adequate funding for a public library.

After the subscription attempt, the Walla Walla Women's Reading Club rallied readers to urge state legislators to pass a bill providing support for cities to establish their own libraries. The bill passed in 1895. What remained to be done was raise funds. At the time, steel-tycoon-turned-philanthropist Andrew Carnegie was giving grants to communities across the nation to build libraries. Whitman College Treasurer Thompson C. Elliott and his wife, Anna Baker Elliott, were key in securing a Carnegie grant. Anna was a daughter of Dorsey Baker and his third wife, Elizabeth. As a sweetener, the Elliotts donated land at Alder and Palouse Streets to build the library. With matching funds in hand, the Reading Club lobbied the city council to create the Walla Walla Public Library. It was dedicated on December 13, 1905.

Patrons and books multiplied at a steady rate. A 1917 report showed that nearly one-quarter of the city's population were "active" readers with the library and the book collection was growing by 10 percent a year. The library was soon storing numerous volumes in every nook and cranny. The building was bulging at the seams.

When the original library was built in 1905, Walla Walla's population was 15,000. By the 1960s, with over 24,000 residents, the city needed, and built, a new library. It was dedicated on June 13, 1970, at its current 238 E. Alder Street location. The former library building was leased by several art groups and began a new chapter in 1971 as the Carnegie Art Center, with a mission to advance the visual arts through classes and art shows.

Today, the library enjoys strong support, with 62 percent of local residents as cardholders. And the library isn't just a place for books. With a full schedule of weekly programs, it is a gathering spot for ideas, discussions, learning, and demonstrations of art and music

The original Walla Walla Public Library was built in 1905 with a grant from steel tycoon Andrew Carnegie on land at Alder and Palouse Streets.

A June 1970 Walla Walla Union-Bulletin notice announces the opening of the new, larger Walla Walla Public Library on Alder Street, with U.S. Senator Henry "Scoop" Jackson the dedication speaker.

*Henrietta Baker Kennedy
(1894-1989), granddaughter of
Dorsey S. Baker, during her
Whitman College years, circa 1915.*

*Ruth Baker Kimball
(1910-2000), great-granddaughter
of Dorsey S. Baker.*

HENRIETTA AND RUTH

By Linda Andrews

HENRIETTA BAKER KENNEDY'S stories from the 1974 *Walla Walla Union-Bulletin* show her to be a lifelong student, a woman who traveled a wondrous world in search of knowledge and understanding. At 80 years of age, she wrote of flying in a small plane into Khajuraho, India, "where a primitive airport had been reconditioned for our landing." And she told of visiting the city of Bamiyan, Afghanistan, with its "immense Buddha carved into the cliff," the very Buddha recently reduced to rubble by the Taliban.

Her observations from Kashmir are both glorious and realistic: "There is water, water everywhere—with floating gardens that raise the most delicious fruits and vegetables. Boats laden with flowers, drugs, spices, embroidered dresses and scarves ply the lake and offer their wares." Her delight is evident, as is a sense of foreboding: "We went far into the tribal country from Peshawar in Pakistan, past fortified houses to a village where, with the simplest tool, guns are copied from all over the world." At the end of her travel to the Asian subcontinent she wrote, "I felt I knew less and less about more and more things."

Born in 1894, Henrietta lived to be 94, and shared her sense of wonder in Walla Walla, where she lectured on her travels. Earlier in life, she was the first woman to earn a degree in mathematics from Whitman College, where she also earned a degree in music. During World War II, she taught math at Whitman and was known as a scholar/teacher. After her death, Professor David Stevens said, "She taught us freedom . . . freedom from the constraints of the conventional . . . God painted Henrietta in large strokes."

Her relative who also modeled the spirit of freedom was Ruth Baker Kimball, whose cause was reproductive rights and accessible family-planning services. The Planned Parenthood center is named in her honor. Together they exemplify forward-thinking women who used their talents to reinvest in our community.

for children and adults. "People feel a part of the library," said Beth Hudson, the library's director since 1991. "The public library is a measure of the vibrancy of a community."

An annual series called Big Idea Talks features authors, poets, innovators, scholars, and artists who share their thinking, expertise, and experiences to generate community conversations on national, regional, and local issues of the day. Riley Clubb, a sixth-generation Baker family member and Walla Walla City Council member, is a fan of the forum. "I enjoy hearing what people are working on professionally and their Big Ideas for making our community the best it can be," he said.

Clubb, one of three council members on the Affordable Housing Task Force, gave a Big Idea Talk in June 2018 on affordable housing— housing for which occupants are paying no more than 30 percent of their total income. The forum gave the opportunity for the community to hear about ideas and policies the task force was researching before recommendations were made to the city council, and to ask questions.

"I think the talk at the library helped set the stage for those recommendations and got the ball rolling on support for making neighborhoods diverse, and therefore affordable," said Clubb. In December 2018, the city council unanimously approved a sweeping set of changes to city zoning, land use, and development regulations to increase affordable housing. The following month in Olympia, Clubb presented Walla Walla's plan to state legislators—underscoring that Big Ideas and community conversations are an important catalyst in shaping change.

Library Director Hudson is proud of the role the library plays in facilitating important community conversations. "Within the framework of Big Idea Talks, we explore ideas which can ultimately build the social capital needed for change," said Hudson.

Top: Ben VanDonge reads to his daughter Brienne at the Walla Walla Public Library.

Bottom: Malysse Hughes, a sophomore at Lincoln High School, helps Jake Jerome, three years old, use the 3-D glasses in an interactive exhibit at the Walla Walla Public LIbrary.

WALLA WALLA COMMUNITY COLLEGE

STEVE VANAUSDLE'S LEGACY as Walla Walla Community College president for 32 years was on full display at his retirement celebration on June 3, 2016, outside the administration building along Titus Creek.

It's a legacy that includes the Aspen Institute College Excellence Program in 2013 naming WWCC the best among the nearly 1,200 two-year schools in the nation, with co-winner Santa Barbara City College. Two years before that distinction, President Barack Obama presented VanAusdle with a "Champions of Change" honor for establishing "a culture that fosters innovation and entrepreneurialism on the campuses and in the communities served by the college."

At his retirement party—attended by several hundred well-wishers, including Governor Jay Inslee—the fruits of VanAusdle's leadership were in evidence. Guests sipped College Cellars wines, made by students in the viticulture and enology program, the first in the nation for a community college, and savored hors d'oeuvres prepared by the school's culinary arts students.

A ramble around the 130-acre campus provided more testaments to what Inslee called VanAusdle's "recognized genius," achieved by partnering with the community and local industries to create programs leading to high-paying jobs.

Among them are the John Deere agricultural machinery technical program, launched in 1994, and wind energy and water management technical programs. More recently, in 2014, the campus became home to the Southeast Area Technical Skills Center, which in partnership with school districts prepares students for postsecondary education and entry into high-skill, high-demand careers.

"Walla Walla Community College's greatest strength is developing students for jobs and helping to drive growth in the regional job market," the Aspen Institute said in awarding WWCC its 2013 prize. "By adding new programs and trimming others based on which programs will provide the best opportunity for employment and good wages, Walla Walla helps students obtain degrees that translate into genuine opportunity."

Aspen also noted WWCC's high student graduation and transfer rates to four-year colleges and universities through its personal, academic, and career advising effort to counsel students on program selection and track progress to a degree. "These programs have led Walla Walla students, many of whom are the first in their family to attend college, to achieve graduation and transfer rates well over the national community college average."

To VanAusdle, "It is all about student success, and investing in strategies that help us do a better job in helping students finish what they start."

Walla Walla Community College President Steve VanAusdle accepts the 2013 Aspen Prize for Community College Excellence from Dr. Jill Biden, wife of then-U.S. Vice President Joe Biden.

ORCHESTRATING A LEGACY

Two years after the public library opened, the city had another asset underway to advance arts and culture in the community, the Walla Walla Symphony. In its 112th year in 2019, it is known as the oldest continuously operating orchestra west of the Mississippi River.

Music teacher and author Dan Shultz wrote about the history of the Symphony's first 100 years in his 2006 book *A Dream Fulfilled*. He described the Symphony's formation as taking shape after local businessman Oliver Beatty attended a fall 1906 performance of an orchestra in Boise, Idaho.

"'Why not in Walla Walla' flashed through his mind and then persisted as he journeyed home," Shultz wrote of Beatty's enthusiasm. "Certainly, if Boise, a city of the same size but with fewer resources, could field an orchestra, Walla Walla, with its four theater orchestras all manned by professional musicians combined with the music resources of the Whitman Conservatory of Music, Walla Walla College music department and local music schools, could do the same."

Beatty shared his idea with others, and by July 1907 the Walla Walla Symphony Club Board of Directors had formed. Its stated goals were to support and present performances of a symphony comprised of local musicians, and to arrange concerts by visiting artists of renown.

Edgar Fischer, who had resigned from the Whitman conservatory to start his own music school, agreed to conduct the club's first performance. It was held at the Keylor Grand Theatre on December 12, 1907. Fischer contacted local musicians and stitched together a small, 29-piece orchestra—7 women and 22 men. They opened the concert with Mozart's *Magic Flute* overture and took the audience through classical works of Beethoven, Grieg, and others. One of the pieces performed, "Serenade," was written by Gena Branscombe, a Whitman College teacher.

The Walla Walla Symphony Orchestra, founded in 1907, performs in the original Walla Walla High School's auditorium in 1960.

Before the first season ended, the board had worked with Whitman College to bring the New York Symphony Orchestra to town for a February concert. The season closed with the noted German chorus The Maennerchor performing with the Walla Walla Symphony under Fischer's direction.

"And what a remarkable first year it had been," Shultz wrote, "a stellar beginning for the symphony club and for its orchestra, an ensemble that would in future years become a crown jewel in the cultural life of Walla Walla." Indeed it did, with musical performances reaching out to all segments of the community and into its public schools, with musicians inspiring youth to study music and fostering succeeding generations of symphony performers.

The symphony performed at various venues, including the Keylor Grand and the Whitman College Chapel. It found a more permanent home in 1928 in the auditorium of the original Walla Walla High School, built in 1916 on Park Street, two blocks south of the college. It continued there until relocating in 1968 to the newly built Cordiner Hall on Whitman's campus.

Its namesake was Walla Walla native Ralph Cordiner, a Whitman alumnus who became president, CEO, and board chairman of General Electric. The corporation donated $500,000 to the $1.6 million performance hall, featuring a large, deep stage, sophisticated acoustics, and a 1,300-seat capacity.

Financing programs had been a tenuous proposition for the symphony board from the beginning. According to Shultz, difficulties were moderated somewhat by musicians volunteering their time for rehearsals and performances, conductors being paid a minimum stipend, and featured soloists playing for free or reduced fees. In 1968, however, it established a trust fund managed by Baker Boyer Bank and launched a campaign to raise $100,000. The symphony gained more solid footing and was able to pay musicians a stipend and further broaden its scope.

According to Leah Wilson-Velasco, symphony CEO since 2011, the endowment had grown to approximately $1.5 million by 2019. Operating expenses are covered by patron subscriptions that had grown to 715 for the 2018-2019 season, individual concert tickets, corporate sponsorships of performances, and printed program advertising by local and regional businesses.

The symphony's longest- and still-serving director and conductor, Yaacov Bergman, was hired in 1987 from a pool of 100 applicants, including several from Europe. His innovative leadership heralded a new era as the symphony increased its number of performances per season and commissioned and premiered original works by local composers. Several of the pieces have been played at Carnegie Hall in New York and by other major metropolitan symphonies Bergman has guest conducted around the nation, Europe, and Asia. He also incorporated more choral, ballet, and operatic works on the symphony stage and, staying in step with developing technology, used visual backdrops to accompany music. The symphony also books special acts to attract diverse audiences and people interested in more than classical music. The Vienna Boys' Choir,

A 1987 Walla Walla Union-Bulletin *article profiles Maestro Yaacov Bergman* as the newly hired conductor of the Walla Walla Symphony Orchestra.

Yaacov Bergman conducts the Walla Walla Symphony in a recent performance.

Walla Walla Symphony trumpeter Gary Gemberling helps Juli Samford, 5, play a few notes while her dad, Wade, encourages her during an afternoon Instrument Petting Zoo prior to a free family concert at Cordiner Hall in Walla Walla, Washington. 2018.

Peking Acrobats, Canadian Brass, and the O'Connor Band have been featured over the years. The Villalobos Brothers commanded the stage in February 2019 for the symphony's annual free show for children and families.

Bergman said what inspired him to study music is what he wants passed on to others, especially children, encouraging them to pursue the joys and structure and shared experience of live music, regardless of its genre. Growing up on an agricultural kibbutz in his native Israel, Bergman said, he loved to sing. "My first music teacher said, 'You have a good ear, you better do something with that,' " he recalled, adding that the instructor then assigned various instruments for him to learn. He pursued his music career in schools in Jerusalem and New York, and with private study under Leonard Bernstein. He said, "It was inspiring and rewarding to realize the extent of my responsibility to make a community appreciate and grow with what you are doing."

Bergman said he accepted his position with the Walla Walla Symphony because the community's agricultural economy reminds him of his boyhood kibbutz, and because of the orchestra's reputation for high-quality performances, broad support, and willingness to "stretch" to try new things.

"I always brag about this place," he said. "It has all the qualities one could look for in life: its three colleges—Whitman, Walla Walla University, and community college—the natural beauty and culture. And without the provincialism you find in other places."

GENTLEMEN OF THE ROAD STOPOVER

Mumford & Sons headline at the main venue, 2015.

WALLA WALLA HAD shown it could attract and accommodate influxes of out-of-town music lovers with its annual chamber music and blues guitar festivals, each performed at several venues in and around the city. But the town's can-do, innovative spirit was put to a supreme test when British folk rock artists Mumford & Sons approached city officials about holding one of the band's five Gentlemen of The Road Stopovers in the United States and United Kingdom in 2015. The two-day music festivals focus on towns not normally toured by major bands and have a vibe for food, the arts, and a welcoming culture.

City Manager Nabiel Shawa recalled what initially motivated the band's promoters, New York-based Madison House Presents, to consider Walla Walla: It was on the list of the National Trust for Historic Preservation's Great American Main Street award winners. "From that lead they dug further and, using Google Earth, scoped out our town and determined how and exactly where the festival could be held in Walla Walla," Shawa said.

The question, however, was whether the town's infrastructure could host a festival that also included Seattle's Foo Fighters and other name acts sharing the marquee, plus dozens of local and regional bands performing on three stages set up on downtown streets. Moreover, could the town of about 30,000 people accommodate a near doubling of its population by concert-goers during the August 14-15 festival?

The answer to both questions was a resounding yes when city officials publicly announced the proposition in March at a gathering of media, local government officials, and business. "It was a knockout," Elio Agostini, then the executive director of the

Downtown Walla Walla Foundation, said in an email to the promoters after the announcement. "Nearly 200 people showed up. . . . It seemed that nobody wanted to leave. They just wanted to hear as much as they could about the Stopover. . . . And lots of questions, and no negative stuff."

Then began months of planning and preparation as the city, merchants, and health and emergency services representatives swung into action to ensure the $7 million to $10 million tourism bonanza would succeed with minimum disruption to the daily rhythms of residents' lives. Madison House covered the city's cost of providing public safety and other services for the event.

The main concert was held at Whitman College's athletic fields, a short walk from downtown as well as the city's municipal golf course, a large part of which was designated as temporary campground and parking lot for fans arriving from around the United States, Canada, and beyond. Main Street from Second Avenue to Palouse Street was cordoned off and turned into a music mall featuring the many local and regional bands on street stages. Merchants and restaurants stocked up, with many making more than a week's worth of typical summer sales in two days.

In the end, talk of the success of the festival was on the lips of the community, visitors, and musicians alike. Said Ben Lovett, Mumford & Sons keyboardist: "It's a really special part of the world, you know."

A large crowd enjoys the music on the *First Avenue Stage* in downtown Walla Walla, 2015.

VISIONS FOR THE VISUAL ARTS

In a 1996 John Muir Publications book by John Villani, *The 100 Best Small Art Towns in America*, Walla Walla was named one of the best for its creative community, fresh air, and affordable living. The community's three colleges had long offered a broad range of art and sculpture to be seen at exhibits and on campus grounds.

But it also had a small foundry started in 1980 by Mark Anderson, a Walla Walla native and Whitman College contemporary arts graduate who would build it into an international treasure used by renowned metal sculptors. In the 1990s, his Walla Walla Foundry was also a major resource in the development of the town's public art scene.

After graduating from Whitman in December 1977, Anderson began teaching art part-time at both Walla Walla Community College and Walla Walla College, now Walla Walla University. He also continued for a few years to set up exhibits at the Sheehan Gallery in Whitman's Olin Hall, where an exhibit by Bay Area sculptor Manuel Neri, known for his life-size sculptures of the human form, turned out to be a "fortuitous" encounter. "I really responded to his art," Anderson said, "and I asked him if I could do any of his work in bronze." Neri, at the time an art professor at the University of California, Davis, gave him a few small plaster figures, which Anderson took to his then-1,000-square-foot foundry he had set up with equipment he'd built.

"The timing was perfect," Anderson said, explaining that Neri's popularity was ascending and "what really sold were his bronzes." The flow of work Neri sent Anderson to cast helped put the foundry on solid financial footing. It also connected Anderson with several more California sculptors whom Neri knew, followed by sculptor Jim Dine, whose towering trio of bronzed Venus de Milos, called "Looking Toward the Avenue," was installed in 1989 near the Museum of Modern Art in Manhattan. Today, there is hardly a continent without an artist, not to mention several local ones, whose privately and publicly displayed works were cast at the Walla Walla Foundry. Anderson's business as of 2019 employed more than 110 people, from management to designers, architects, engineers, model makers, fabricators, structural welders, and sculpture trainees.

But it wasn't until 1991 that Anderson discovered that his hometown, too, had a thirst for public art. That year the foundry completed Ed Kienholz's replica of a full hunting camp that the Idaho installation artist and assemblage sculptor used near his home near Lake Pend Oreille. It featured in fine detail such things as an old pickup truck, a gutted deer hanging from a tree, and a man sitting by

Walla Walla native Mark Anderson in 1996 at the Walla Walla Foundry. Started in 1980, his foundry has been used for decades by world-class metal sculptors for creating private and public pieces.

a fireplace—all bronzed. Anderson asked Kienholz if he could put it on public display for a day in the courtyard of his foundry before packing it up and shipping it. He agreed, and with only a day's advance notice more than 500 people came to see it.

A week later, he said, Rob Robinson and Jeana Garske, who were part of a group forming an arts alliance to promote public art and arts education in Walla Walla, came to his office and asked him to join. "So I thought about it," Anderson said, "and with my business career I worked for all these artists outside the area. But it's nice to maybe see what I could do from my community, so I became one of the members."

The nonprofit organization, Blue Mountain Arts Alliance, now ArtWalla, officially formed in 1992. Its initial mission was to promote public art and arts education in the city. With grants from the local Sherwood Trust to buy public art, the alliance held competitions among artists, donated chosen works to the city, and worked with the parks department and city council on placement. It has since expanded its mission to be a support and networking entity for individual artists and other visual and performing arts organizations in Walla Walla.

Its first major project, in 1993, was to save the ornate upper two stories of the 1902 Odd Fellows Temple's sandstone façade before the building was demolished for a parking lot. Underwritten by Baker Boyer, the $70,000 project required dismantling the façade stone by stone and marking each for reassembly on the west wall of a Main Street building adjacent to Heritage Park. In 1997, the façade's 20 panels that were once windows on the temple became a work called "Windows on the Past," each a colorful porcelain and steel-bordered photographic image of historical people and ethnic groups that made the valley from 1850 through 1950. Anderson's foundry, along with project director Jeanne McMenemy, photographer Hans Matschukat, and research interns from Whitman College and Walla Walla University, contributed to the public artwork.

A 1993 Blue Mountain Arts Alliance project allowed for the dismantling and saving of the sandstone façade of the 1902 Odd Fellows Temple. Before the building was razed, the façade was moved stone by stone and reassembled in downtown Walla Walla's Heritage Park as a public art installation called "Windows on the Past."

CHICKEN AND THE EGG

WAYNE CHABRE AND Jeanne McMenemy's 2004 bronze sculpture *A Delicate Balance* is among many works of public art installed throughout Walla Walla. "Humor is one response in the face of our concerns," Chabre said of the piece, cast at the Walla Walla Foundry. "In this piece, the chickens balance precariously on hatching eggs to playfully present the age-old question: 'Which came first, the chicken or the egg?' but also to help us think about our 'delicate balance' in the world."

As of 2019, ArtWalla recorded 23 public sculptures in downtown Walla Walla and on the Whitman campus, many of which were fabricated at the Walla Walla Foundry. Other sculptures include Walla Walla painter and sculptor Jeffrey Hill's bronzes, homages to wheat farmers and vineyard workers that, respectively, grace private property in the center of downtown and outside Walla Walla Community College's wine education center.

Anderson said public art brings more to Walla Walla than just interesting pieces of art to see; it gives a personality, a sharing of ideas among generations, and a voice to the community.

"What it brings is discussion," he said. "There's always debate—I think that's healthy. So what we added to our culture was the ability to have that discussion. Why do I like this piece? Why don't I? Do we have more? And it integrated into an evolution of this old city re-creating itself as a place welcoming to outsiders."

And the pieces will endure time and weather for the many decades to come, he added. "It's really built to last generations. We all felt like we were doing something that would stand the test of time. We had influenced the community in the right way—in a way that would build community."

It's not only Walla Walla's parks and streetscapes where residents and visitors can view and contemplate a vibrant palette of local art. The walls of wine-tasting rooms, restaurants, and coffee shops also serve as galleries for local painters, photographers, and crafts artists to show and sell their work.

Anderson is intrigued by the caliber of artists who live in Walla Walla. "I don't think many people in Walla Walla realize how many artists there are and how much work is sold outside Walla Walla." While inspiration is personal for each artist, Anderson is influenced by the landscape and the character of the small town. "I love the landscape," he said. "I just love the feel. I can sense the character of the town and the people, which is unusual for a small town. I know that from traveling—this is a special place."

Bronze sculpture Thoughts Discovered, *on First Avenue and Main Street, was created by Walla Walla sculptor Brad Rude in 2001.*

Community leaders and state officials cut the ribbon during a ceremony in 2007 to open Walla Walla Community College's William A. Grant Water & Environmental Center.

CHAPTER 8

Public Service and The Walla Walla Way

"On this day, March 8, 2002, the undersigned pledge to work together, within the form of the Walla Walla Watershed Alliance, to restore and maintain the ecological, cultural, and economic health of the Walla Walla Basin. We make this commitment on behalf of the future for the next seven generations and beyond. A promise made is a promise kept."

— The Walla Walla Promise

Sometimes heard in Walla Walla over a glass of wine or while seated around a conference table is the statement: What we do together we do best.

"There is an unusually high degree of collaboration in the valley," said Nabiel Shawa, city manager of Walla Walla since 2009, with 37 years in local governments across the state. "It's just part of the culture."

Historically, the remoteness of the settlement may have set a tone of collaboration. "If we want a library district, if we want a landfill, if we want roads built, we've got to come together and figure it out," said Shawa. The wisdom of the valley focused on the betterment of all.

"Yes, we compete with each other. No, we do not see eye to eye on every issue by any stretch," said Shawa. "This is not Shangri-La. This is real."

While individual entities might poke around the edges of an issue, the broader question "What do we need to do collaboratively?" gets to a bigger and better solution, and actually resolves the issue. "And that's The Walla Walla Way," said Megan Clubb. "It's collaboration at a community-wide level. And the value of it is that you actually solve these really contentious, sticky community problems."

The blue-shaded area in this U.S. Army Corps of Engineers overview shows the area through
Walla Walla at risk of flooding should the Mill Creek dam, levee, and concrete channel system fail.

This multigenerational practice of people working collaboratively in the community could be called a mindset or a vibe. The Mill Creek Coalition, the Blue Mountain Community Foundation, the Walla Walla Watershed Alliance, and the SOS Clinic are just several illustrations of The Walla Walla Way in action.

MILL CREEK COALITION

In the fall of 2013, Mark Kajita and port commissioners Mike Fredrickson and Paul Schneidmiller, as well as President of the Downtown Walla Walla Foundation Tom Baffney, set such a vibe stirring over martinis. Or so the story goes. Their musings initiated an endeavor to resolve an infrastructure issue that threatened the very foundations of Walla Walla.

Through the heart of the city of Walla Walla runs a seven-mile levee embankment and concrete channel owned and operated by the Walla Walla County Flood Control District. With an assessed property value of approximately $3 billion within the Mill Creek Flood Control Zone, the channel protects nearly 20,000 people and 6,000 structures including schools, colleges, hospitals, and the award-winning historic downtown commercial core. Spanning the channel at various points are city-owned bridges and parking structures, as well as buildings owned by the private sector. While the county owns and maintains the structure, designed to contain surging water in a flood event, the flow of water is controlled by the U.S. Army Corps of Engineers.

Mill Creek is situated at the base of the Blue Mountains, with a 97-square-mile watershed. It directs water from springs, rain, and snowmelt from the Walla Walla basin on a course for the Columbia River.

In February 1996, a rapid temperature rise, combined with a rain-on-snow event, caused the water within the channel to run through the city at 4,100 cubic feet per second (cfs). The creek overflowed its banks upstream of Walla Walla and damaged levees. As the water raged, some downtown businesses with basements were flooded, and the city closed streets to protect the structural integrity of certain bridges.

For 48 hours the Corps diverted 2,200 cfs of floodwater above the city into Bennington Lake Reservoir, reducing the natural peak from approximately 6,000 cfs closer to the downstream channel design capacity of 3,500 cfs. But the reservoir rapidly filled to capacity.

Mark Kajita recalled standing on a bridge at First and Main, watching the surging water, thinking the bridge could collapse. "There was palpable fear in the community during '96 because the water was getting so close to overflowing that we realized we just dodged a bullet," he said.

Although flows dropped below 1,400 cfs after three days—signaling the end of the flood-management event—mounting concern within the community focused on one question: Was the aging control channel up to handling another flood event, or worse, an event like the 1931 flood?

Images from the March 1931 flood show water from Mill Creek flowing through the streets of Walla Walla, flooding businesses and residential areas. Receding floodwaters revealed extensive damage to state and county highways and bridges, streets, buildings, and railroad

This map shows the 36-square-mile upper portion of the Mill Creek Watershed, which supplies drinking water to the City of Walla Walla. The entire watershed is 97 square miles.

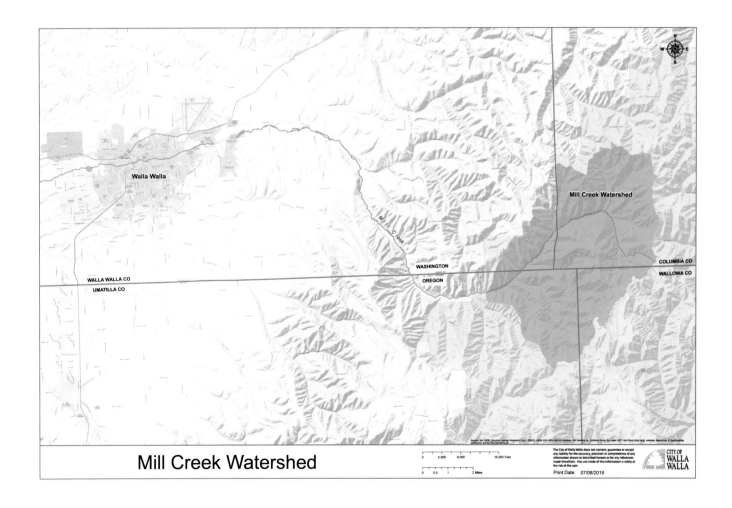

Mill Creek Watershed

1931 WALLA WALLA FLOOD

beds, as well as heavy loss of farmland and livestock. Destruction caused by the flood was the catalyst for the construction of the current Mill Creek flood-control project.

Congress passed the Flood Control Acts of 1938 and 1941 authorizing the construction of the Mill Creek Control Plan and the Mill Creek Channel. The U.S. Army Corps of Engineers completed construction in 1948. The system was composed of an off-channel storage reservoir—later named "Virgil B. Bennington Lake"—three diversion works, two dams, outlet works, and nearly eight miles of leveed and concrete flood channel.

Nearly 60 years later, amidst growing concern that the channel was reaching the end of its design life, the Corps, the county, and the city conducted independent studies on the aging infrastructure. Then, after an annual inspection of bridges in 2012, the city used cyclone fencing to block a portion of a parking lot that spanned Mill Creek on Second and Rose, concluding it was not safe for vehicle traffic. Assessed channel deterioration also resulted in load restrictions and vehicle rerouting in the area.

In 1996, the channel did exactly what it was supposed to do—prevent flooding and the destruction of life and property. But its ability to do so again was suspect. "If we were to have a significant flood event similar to the 1930s, it would wipe out our economy for at least 12 to 18 months, and maybe longer," said Shawa. "How many businesses can survive that kind of impact?"

Not only would impacted businesses struggle to rebuild and restore inventory, but they would struggle to pay taxes. In a sales- and property-tax-

Walla Walla streets and bridges downtown and in residential areas were awash in torrents of floodwaters when a combination of heavy rains and rapid snowmelt caused Mill Creek to jump its banks in March 1931.

based economy, government entities would lack cash flow to maintain operations, including the repair of damaged streets and structures.

Flood devastation would interrupt Walla Walla's annual $130 million tourism economy. Regional tourism is founded on repeat tourists and the relationships they build with winemakers, shop owners, and restaurants. "Relationships with winemakers, that great restaurant we went to, that wonderful little soap shop, those all build memories and people come back and want to revisit those," said Shawa. An interruption in the tourism cycle for one to two years could be costly. "There is no guarantee they will return when we are back open for business," said Shawa.

Conversation about the impact of a potential failure of the flood-control structure was ramping up at the city, county, port, the Corps, and the Downtown Foundation. But there was a problem. With federal, county, and city involvement with private sector overlay, no one entity was in control. "What we didn't have at that point was the unifying body to come together to figure out the strategy in which to effect the necessary changes," said Shawa.

In 2013, Kajita—with the support of the Baker Boyer Board—decided to be a catalyst for the formation of a unified body committed to collaborating over a number of years to tackle the issue. Along with the help of Frederickson and Schneidmiller, Kajita brought together a team from the city, county, port, and eventually the Confederated Tribes of the Umatilla Indian Reservation and the Corps. They shared a common goal to solve the flood-control issue.

"Mark, in the spirit of public service, seeing this real challenge, decided to step forward and really elevate the conversation," said Shawa. "And that was the genesis of the Mill Creek Coalition."

At the first meeting, Kajita remembered, they sat around a table at Baker Boyer establishing a core commitment to leave the community in a better position. "And then I said, 'Can we also admit that this is going to be a long process where some of our constituencies may not be in favor of what we're doing, but it's for the greater good?' " said Kajita. "And, 'Can we all agree that we are doing this so our kids and grandkids have the privilege to call Walla Walla home?' And we all said yes. That was one of the proudest days of my life."

Because the flood zone included federal infrastructure, it would literally take an act of Congress and a signature from the President of the United States to secure funding to initiate studies on the aging system.

The first task was to request an appraisal study by the Corps on the aging infrastructure. This was requested on April 8, 2014, and completed in October. The Corps documented "changed conditions" including deficiencies in levees, floodwalls, and drainage systems. The Corps recommended initiation of a General Investigation Study focused on risk assessment of flooding, and risk to life and safety associated with the flood channel. The study would cost $3 million, half to be paid by local sources and half by the federal government.

The coalition faced two obstacles: securing local funding and competing nationally for the federal authorization of funds. "It was a five-year process that actually involved two separate acts of Congress to get us funds that we needed to start the study," said Kajita. Coalition members first agreed on an interlocal cost-sharing plan, each member tasked with securing budget approval from their respective board, committee, or council. The next step: petition Washington, D.C.

With a commitment of firm local funding and request for a federal match, the coalition made bi-annual trips to D.C. "It is a powerful statement when you are standing in front of congressional officials back in D.C., when you physically have the port, the city, the county, and the private sector together," said Shawa, "and you are physically standing shoulder to shoulder." The group had a compelling message of public and private institutions working together to protect an award-winning community that was at risk of being annihilated by a flood that could easily be prevented.

"We petitioned them for five years until they said, 'Okay, we'll do a study and think through what a redesign would be,' " said Kajita. In 2018, the Mill Creek Flood Control Project was one of only six studies authorized nationally.

The study will examine the economy of the region, the threat of loss of life, as well as the impact on Mid-Columbia steelhead and bull trout, two species of fish protected by the Endangered Species Act. As currently designed, the channel and fish ladders act as a passage barrier four to six months of the year, and conditions within the channel create temperatures in Mill Creek that are lethal to the ESA-listed fish. The channel has been identified by regional fisheries managers as one of five critical impediments to the recovery of Mid-Columbia steelhead across the Columbia Basin.

The discussion about fish passage brought the Confederated Tribes to the table. "They were trying to solve fish, we were trying to solve flooding, but either way it would involve the federal government," said Kajita.

Other citizen groups have added to the conversation by organizing community meetings to discuss possible ways to increase the aesthetics and recreational uses of the leveed and concrete channel. Since safety, not aesthetics, is the primary objective of the Corps-controlled federal funding, the coalition is working with the Corps to design a channel that would allow for future recreational and aesthetic improvements, called bolt-on amenities.

Kajita is proud of the collaborative work of the coalition to rally community, state, and federal support. "One of the things that I'm most proud of that I've done at the bank," he said, "is to use the resources of the bank to bring people together to solve something that was really unsolvable by any one organization."

U.S. Rep. Cathy McMorris Rodgers (center) and Walla Walla area leaders met in February 2019 to build support for the repair and improvement of the aging Mill Creek channel. (From left) Port of Walla Walla Commissioner Michael Fredrickson, Baker Boyer President and CEO Mark Kajita, Walla Walla County Commissioner Jim Johnson, McMorris Rodgers, Walla Walla City Councilman Jerry Cummins, City Manager Nabiel Shawa, and Port of Walla Walla Executive Director Patrick Reay.

WALLA WALLA WATERSHED ALLIANCE

FOR MORE THAN 100 years, the Walla Walla River and area streams ran dry each summer. This seasonal dewatering of waterways occurred from the late 1880s and throughout the 20th century as the area population and agricultural development demanded more water from streams to support the community and economy. With the turn-of-the-century focus on restoring endangered fish species in the West, water users and environmental interests needed to reach a compromise to restore stream flows.

Megan Clubb remembered the day Bob Rupar, former VP of marketing at Nelson Irrigation and partner in Pepper Bridge and SeVein Vineyards; and Ron Brown, GM at Earl Brown & Sons and owner, Blue Mountain Cider and Watermill Winery, came into her office to ask her to join an alliance to tackle the water resource problem in the valley. What hooked her was the fact that they already had at the table farmers, environmentalists, and representatives from the Confederated Tribes. What they needed: a representative from the business community.

Clubb already knew how important water was for the future of the Walla Walla Valley. In 2002, she joined with key community leaders to launch the Walla Walla Watershed Alliance. To formalize a cooperative, problem-solving approach, Alliance members including landowners, environmentalists, Tribal representatives, and community leaders committed themselves to the Walla Walla Promise:

On this day, March 8, 2002, the undersigned pledge to work together, within the form of the Walla Walla Watershed Alliance, to restore and maintain the ecological, cultural, and economic health of the Walla Walla Basin. We make this commitment on behalf of the future for the next seven generations and beyond. A promise made is a promise kept.

The Alliance researched new ways to efficiently manage water, and it employed flexibility and shared governance to balance the resource needs of fish and irrigators. This unique approach and cooperation in problem solving among all of the partnering entities in the Walla Walla Watershed resulted in unprecedented approval through state legislation in 2009 to pilot local water management with irrigators, environmentalists, and tribal and community leaders partnering to find a balance.

"The Alliance's innovative efforts paved the way for stakeholders to work together, putting local people in control of their own destiny with the 2009 formation of the Walla Walla Watershed Management Partnership," said Cathy Schaeffer, former executive director of the Walla Walla Watershed Alliance and Walla Walla Watershed Management Partnership. "The Partnership's success and shared learning continues even today, providing a model for collaboration in addressing water resource challenges."

From left to right:

Greg Tompkins,* Commissioner
Walla Walla County Board of Commissioners
Frank Chopp, Speaker
WA State House of Representatives
Kevin Scribner*
Salmon-Safe and Walla Walla Watershed Alliance
Jay Manning, Director
WA State Department of Ecology
Bill Grant, Representative and Majority Caucus Chairman
WA State House of Representatives
Bob Rupar,* Vice President
Nelson Irrigation
Jon McFarland, Chair
Walla Walla Community College Board of Trustees
Maureen Walsh, Representative
WA State House of Representatives
Megan Clubb,* President and CEO
Baker Boyer Bank
Paul Schneidmiller, President
Port of Walla Walla Commission
Antone Minthorn, Chair
Confederated Tribes of the Umatilla Indian Reservation Board of Trustees
Steve VanAusdle,* President
Walla Walla Community College
Cathy Schaeffer,* Executive Director
Walla Walla Watershed Alliance

(*) member of the Walla Walla Watershed Alliance

Walla Walla Watershed Alliance members not pictured: Ron Brown (Earl Brown and Sons), N. Kathryn Brigham (Confederated Tribes of the Umatilla Indian Reservation), Pat McConnell (Walla Walla County Conservation District), Duane Cole and Hal Thomas (City of Walla Walla), Lisa Pelly (Trout Unlimited Washington Water Project), Dick Ducharme (Columbia County Landowner)

BLUE MOUNTAIN COMMUNITY FOUNDATION

It began with an initial gift of $100,000 and now annually gives away over $2 million; the Blue Mountain Community Foundation is the story of four local individuals who secured the collaboration of a community.

In 1984, Pete Peery was running the trust department at Baker Boyer Bank. He knew he lived in a generous community that was interested in solving local issues, and he wanted to find a way to facilitate this. Peery wasn't alone; estate-planning attorney John Reese, superintendent of the Walla Walla school district F.B. "Pete" Hanson, and banker L.E. "Lou" Keiler shared Peery's interest. They knew that when people were deciding what to do with their assets—especially their estates—the primary regional philanthropic options were giving to Whitman College or to the Shriners hospital in Spokane. While both were worthy causes, the four envisioned creating a new way for people to put money to work locally for the causes they care about. They decided to start a community foundation focused on growing a large endowment.

An endowment would secure the opportunity for donors to achieve their philanthropic goals in perpetuity. The foundation would manage the investment of donor funds to grow the principal and annually distribute a percentage of the earnings to specific causes as directed by the donor. Megan Clubb firmly believes in the power of a community foundation to support local causes. "Way beyond my lifetime, in perpetuity, I can leave money to this incredible organization and their mission will be fulfilled by my support for years to come," she said.

But starting a community foundation is expensive. "Foundations need scale. They need a lot of money," said Lawson Knight, director of the Blue Mountain Community Foundation from 2002 to 2013. He quickly calculated at his desk: a one percent service fee on $100,000 is $1,000. "Well, how many people can you pay with $1,000 to do the work? So now you get $1 million. Well, one percent of $1 million is $10,000. You still can't pay staff. So, it takes a lot of money to have the thing operate by itself."

Lacking start-up capital for the foundation, Peery and Reese found another way. Peery advocated within Baker Boyer for utilizing his

Blue Mountain Community Foundation founding trustees were (from left) attorney John M. Reese, executive director Louis E. Keiler, Baker Boyer Bank trust department director W.W. "Pete" Peery, and Foundation board President F.B. "Pete" Hanson.

division to oversee the investments entrusted to the foundation. In 1984, he received support from the Baker Boyer Board to handle the foundation's administrative and investment functions free of charge. "The bank had the expertise in-house to administer and manage the investments, and we were used to filing all the necessary paperwork," said Clubb. "So, basically the bank ran the Blue Mountain Foundation in its infancy. We didn't charge fees." The fledgling foundation operated out of the Baker Boyer building for the next 18 years and functioned with the support of an active board and a part-time administrator, Eleanor Kane.

But Peery and Reese did not rely on Baker Boyer alone; they found individuals and businesses within the community to gift their services. Reese and other attorneys gifted time preparing estate-planning documents, a local accounting firm donated its services, and printing was done free of charge by Inland Saxum Printing. "It was one of the great gifts of Pete Peery to make sure this wasn't a simple Baker Boyer start-up," said Knight, "so he was able to knit the entire financial and legal community in at the start."

In 2002, when the foundation hired its first full-time employee, a director, it already had $13 million in assets. "You have the generosity

Ribbon-cutting ceremony for The Hub, a facility providing services to youth, including an emergency homeless shelter and student health center, September 2017. Officials and members of the local nonprofits that made it happen join in the celebration: (from left) Meagan Anderson-Pira, Children's Home Society of Washington regional director; Stan Ledington, The Health Center director; Kathy Covey, Blue Mountain Action Council CEO; and Tim Meliah, Catholic Charities director.

FINANCIAL LITERACY FOR KIDS IN THE TRI-CITIES

JAN DARRINGTON DOESN'T leave her work—helping clients navigate financial pathways to success—at the office as Baker Boyer Bank's Family Advisor vice president in the Tri-Cities. She also teaches business and life skills to youth as a Junior Achievement (JA) volunteer.

She got involved with JA in 2002 while she was Booster Club president at Kennewick's Southridge High School. She quickly found that JA satisfied her desire to teach kids, and it dovetailed with her experience as a mom and a Baker Boyer family advisor.

"Junior Achievement offers structured programs that allow me to bring in elements of what I do as a professional," Darrington said. "This includes financial literacy, personal finance, current affairs, and career building."

The Tri-Cities chapter started more than 30 years ago, sending hundreds of volunteers into local classrooms from kindergarten through high school.

Darrington's nearly two decades with JA includes serving three years on the local board. In the Tri-Cities, business advisor Mitch Roach has also been a regular JA volunteer, and nearly a dozen Baker Boyer employees have participated in JA across all of our Eastern Washington locations.

Above: Baker Boyer employees (from left) Kylee Slone, Jan Darrington, Melissa Deming, and Megan Farrow and her husband at the Rodeo Bowl to raise funds for Junior Achievement in 2019.

"There are so many exceptionally talented people who are working on tough community and social issues, and they are open to working with others. That is the core of The Walla Walla Way."

— Megan Clubb

of individuals, of people like John Reese and Pete Peery, who invested their time and energy to get this going," said Clubb.

In 2018, the foundation had a record year, giving away $3.5 million to 162 organizations and 272 student scholarship recipients. Of the nearly $2 million distributed from the endowment, most funds were received by local charities. Looking through the recipient list, it is hard to find a local nonprofit that has not received a contribution from the foundation.

Kari Isaacson, executive director since 2012, is proud of the impact of the endowment on regional causes across various sectors, including programs that target at-risk youth. In 2018, a grant given by the foundation assisted a partnership of five local organizations to build a facility called The Hub. The partnership of nonprofits worked together to achieve their dream of a shared center that provides significant services to youth in the community, including an emergency shelter for homeless youth and a state-of-the-art Student Health Center.

Area students are getting a better chance at higher education as well. "Most awards are to students who have significant financial need. The average scholarship is touching $2,000, which is two-thirds annual tuition at the community college," said Knight. "These are important amounts to help students."

Giving USA conducted a research study focused on philanthropy that compared per capita giving in counties across America. Walla Walla County gives at a higher rate than most. "We have a population that is disproportionately generous," said Knight.

Walla Walla's relative per capita endowment is also significantly higher than that of other counties in Washington. Knight likens the endowment to an aquifer that has the capacity to replenish and strengthen a community through good times and bad. "When most people are giving away hundreds or a few thousand dollars, to have an institution that can give away hundreds of thousands of dollars in the community is significant," said Knight. "That is the other great insight Pete had: he knew the effect of compounding and the power of endowments—that the real power of the organization was not going to be in its first few years but a generation away."

EVERYBODY AT THE TABLE

"There are so many exceptionally talented people who are working on tough community and social issues," said Clubb, "and they are open to working with others. That is the core of The Walla Walla Way."

Addressing issues on the scale of natural resource conflict and shared infrastructure, or among at-risk populations, requires a high-level understanding of the complexity of the issue and the ability to execute a solution holistically. "You can't solve these problems and improve the community without knowing the cause," said Clubb. "Equally important, once you have a solution and you are executing on a plan, it must be holistic and engage all stakeholders."

A collaborative approach to both understanding community problems and executing solutions is The Walla Walla Way. "One of the big advantages of a community our size is that collaborative efforts go a long way toward solving problems," said Clubb. "With a small team of people in this community, it is amazing what can be accomplished."

VITAL WINES AND
THE SOS CLINIC
WITH ASHLEY TROUT

BY LINDA ANDREWS

A crew picks grapes for Vital Wines.

WHAT DOES IT TAKE to meet a community need? It takes empathy, vision, perhaps personal experience. And certainly a vitality of spirit. Ashley Trout, a major force behind the SOS Health Services Clinic, embodies all those characteristics.

The SOS Clinic, a free, nonprofit health care clinic in the Walla Walla area, works to meet the needs of the uninsured and under-insured regardless of citizenship status, location, or income. That the clinic exists is a marvel of collaboration. It was founded by a service-minded local physician and is staffed by volunteer physicians, nurses, students, phlebotomists, translators, and transcriptionists. SonBridge Community Center donates space. A full-time AmeriCorps member handles schedules and helps with daily operations. And Ashley Trout donates 100 percent of the profits from her Vital Wines to the clinic.

Ashley Trout, founder of Vital Wines.

Ashley Trout came to this project through her concern for vineyard workers, whose labor is physical and often strenuous. They are also often uninsured and unsure of where to seek care. Trout, the daughter of a surgeon, was privileged to grow up with the domestic help of a Spanish-speaking woman she calls her "surrogate grandmother." Trout remembered translating for her at medical appointments and seeing other children struggle to represent their loved ones in that fraught and crucial environment. Later, after graduating from Whitman College, Trout spent time in Japan and was seriously injured in a rock-climbing accident. Because she was in Japan on a work visa, her weeks-long hospital stay and multiple surgeries were covered by Japan's national health-care system.

Trout returned to Walla Walla informed by those experiences. When she became part of the wine industry, she had the motivation and passion to provide health care for wine workers. As she said, "I understood pretty quickly, looking around the Washington wine industry, who we are, and half of who we are doesn't have health insurance. It's a tough spot, and I wanted to fix that."

Word spread about Vital Wines' mission of "Aiming to improve access to health care for vineyard and cellar workers in our local community," which is realized through the SOS Clinic. The result—greater collaboration between wineries in the form of donated fruit at harvest time, donated labels, corks, shipping supplies, lab work, and barrels. Trout said, "The wine community has just come out of the woodwork to donate." The clinic serves hundreds of patients a quarter, but the work is not done. A need persists for more open hours at the clinic. And, Trout has said, "There really should be a mobile unit in agricultural communities for people who don't have cars or can't afford extra trips for preventive health-care visits."

Because of the talented, determined people of the Valley, Trout's vision continues to effect change. Trout described a circle that feels right—when a community cares for the people who "provide us with beautiful wines," those wines can be enjoyed "with pleasure on the palate and the soul."

Afterword

At the top of a faded yellow sheet of paper a tidy, handwritten script notes that July 6, 1988, "will be the 100th anniversary of D.S. Baker's death."

Written by former Baker Boyer Bank President Vernon Kegley—beloved by many as a mentor and friend—the note is a memoir of sorts, reflecting on the legacy of D.S. Baker and the bank he founded in 1869. "Baker Boyer was 50 years old when the present Ford Motor Co. was incorporated in 1919, and when RCA was founded in 1919. We were 100 years old when Albertsons was incorporated in 1969," Kegley wrote.

He then noted the years other large American companies were established after Baker Boyer opened its doors in Walla Walla: Atlantic Richfield (1870), American Telephone and Telegraph (1885), Pacific Power & Light (1910), IBM (1911), DuPont (1915), General Motors (1916), and General Mills (1928).

Kegley reflected that when D.S. Baker established Baker Boyer Bank, the Civil War had ended only four years before, in 1865. Ulysses S. Grant, elected in 1868, was in his first year as president of the United States. The nation was celebrating the opening of the Suez Canal in Egypt. And in Washington Territory, there had yet to be a railroad, telephone, or telegraph.

By the time D.S. Baker died in 1888—at the age of 65 and one year before Washington Territory became a state—Walla Walla had electric lights, a railroad, and a telephone exchange with 16 subscribers, as well as a baseball team. The following year his bank received its national charter and became Baker Boyer National Bank.

The bank was born in an era of rapid innovation, and a legacy of adaptation and partnership is inherent to the DNA of not only Baker Boyer but also Walla Walla and the region. It has been a 150-year journey characterized by entrepreneurialism and collaboration.

"Legacies are created by the journeys that precede them," said Baker Boyer Chair Megan Clubb, a fifth-generation descendant of D.S. Baker. "You can't understand the legacy unless you understand the story of the journey."

In its most rudimentary form, a legacy is a gift of money or property granted to someone in a will, a bequest. But the deeper

For 150 years Baker Boyer has been privileged to play a role in contributing to legacies of communities and creating opportunity for current and future generations to realize their full potential.

meaning of the word implies that what is given has a long-lasting effect on present and future generations. For Walla Walla and the region, legacies are not only gifts of well-tended currency and beloved land, but something more. Locals call that "something" The Walla Walla Way—a collaborative spirit committed to building strong communities.

As you have read the stories of our Baker Boyer Bank family, friends, and clients who have been part of our region's collective journey, we hope you have gained a new appreciation for the culture of Walla Walla and the region, a culture fortified by people truly committed to nurturing the health and vitality of our communities. We hope you will join us in savoring the threads of innovation, entrepreneurialism, and partnership woven through 150 years and across a wide swath of southeast and central Washington.

For 150 years Baker Boyer has been privileged to play a role in contributing to legacies of communities and creating opportunity for current and future generations to realize their full potential. Baker Boyer's unwavering nurturing of the families, businesses, and nonprofits that create the fabric of our region has been our work since the day D.S. Baker opened his second-floor office in 1869, and continues each morning as we open our doors. It is a role marked by steadfast determination to cultivate the best of what this land and its people can offer for the region's future.

Join us in celebrating this milestone, the vitality of the region, and the many people whose energies and generosity of spirit make this a special place.

EMPLOYEES AS FAMILY

It's hard to explain the level of trust, admiration, and respect we have as a bank family. You really have to experience it to believe it!

– Mark Kajita

ACKNOWLEDGMENTS

CREATING A BOOK spanning 150 years of corporate and community history required the help and expertise of many people. We wish to extend our abiding appreciation to those who talked with us, shared their stories and expertise, read parts of our manuscript, shared art and photographs, and led us to sources that have helped tell this story about Baker Boyer, Walla Walla, and the region:

Baker Boyer: Brittney Nelson, Cathy Schaeffer, Cedric Jacobs-Jones, Dave Gordon, Elizabeth Humphrey, Jacki Boatman, Jessica Long, Jim Wilson, Joe Burlingame, John Mathwich, Jon Bren, JT Lieuallen, Judy Hicks, Mark Hess, Mark Kajita, Mark Lutcher, Rachel Kibukevich, Rob Blethen, Rose Hadjuk, Rosendo Guizar, Russ Colombo, Russ Smith, Susie Colombo, Tricia Agee, and Victoria Weeks

Baker Family Members: Cathy Allen, Elizabeth Hill, Gail Kimball, Jeanne Eagleson, Krista Burt, Lynne Bush, Marty Clubb, Megan Clubb, Peter Allen, Riley Clubb, Sander Olson, and Steve Kimball

The Community: Army Corps of Engineers (Alex Colter), ArtWalla (Patty Gardner, Tricia Harding), Blue Mountain Action Council (Kathy Covey), Blue Mountain Community Foundation (Kari Isaacson, Liz McClure), Bygone Walla Walla (Joe Drazan), City of Walla Walla (Nabiel Shawa, Beth Hudson, Mori Struve, Joseph French), Clark Colahan, Doug Crouch, Falkenbergs (Skip Cundiff), Eric Hoverson, Fort Walla Walla Museum (Shannon Buchal, James Payne), H.T. Rea Farming Corp. (Nathan Rea), Ingeniux (Jim Edmunds), Jeffrey Hill, K Vintners (Emily Maze), John Curry Photography, L'Ecole N° 41 (Marty Clubb, Pam Bykonen), Lawson Knight, Leonetti Cellar (Gary, Nancy, Chris, and Amy Figgins), Leslie (Yantis) Brown, Linda Andrews, Mainstem Malt (Phil Neumann), Marcus Whitman Hotel (Dan Leeper, Kyle Mussman), Pepper Bridge Winery & Amavi Cellars (Norm McKibben, Dana Lane), Rick Doyle, Susie Golden, *Tri-City Herald* (Laurie Williams), Visit Walla Walla (Caleb Agee), Vital Wines (Ashley Trout, Sammi Clute), Walla Walla Foundry (Mark Anderson, Glynis McClellan), Walla Walla Portrait Design (Marty Huie), Walla Walla River Packing and Storage (Harry Hamada), Walla Walla Symphony (Leah Wilson-Velasco), *Walla Walla Union-Bulletin* (Brian Hunt, Greg Lehman), Walla Walla Valley Wine Alliance (Ashley Mahan), Whitman Archives (Ben Murphy, Dana Bronson, Joel Gaytan), Whitman Mission National Historic Site (Park Ranger Emily Devereaux), Woodward Canyon (Rick Small, Darcey Fugman-Small)

PUBLICATIONS

Forty Years a Pioneer, W.W. Baker; *Gold, Rawhide and Iron*, Helen Baker Reynolds; *A Dream Fulfilled: One Hundred Years of the Walla Walla Symphony Orchestra*, Dan Shultz; *The Horticultural Heritage of Walla Walla County, 1818-1977*, Joe J. Locati; *Yakima Herald-Republic* archives; *Walla Walla Union-Bulletin* archives; *The Walla Walla Story: Washington Centennial Edition*, Vance Orchard.

SPECIAL THANKS

We would like to extend a special thanks to the following people for extensively sharing photographs from their archives that add richer texture to the telling of this story: Greg Lehman

With special thanks to the Baker Boyer family of employees.

(Greg Lehman Photography and the *Walla Walla Union-Bulletin*); Brian Hunt (*Walla Walla Union-Bulletin*); Ben Murphy, Dana Bronson, and Joel Gaytan (Whitman Archives); and Shannon Buchal and James Payne (Fort Walla Walla Museum).

A huge thank-you to Petyr Beck and his team at Documentary Media. Petyr's keen sense for storytelling—both written and visual—as well as his attention to detail and his collaborative approach made all the difference in this project. We gratefully acknowledge the work of Tori Smith and Edward Daschle, the keen editing eye of Judy Gouldthorpe, and the talent of designer Marilyn Esguerra.

Thomas P. Skeen has a few personal thank-yous, starting with Megan Clubb and Mark Kajita, for their conception of the book and selfless insistence that it accent the community's achievements, not just the bank's 150-year role in Walla Walla. To Petyr Beck, Kelly Black, Rob Blethen, and Jim

Wilson, for putting their faith and trust in him for this project, and their support and wise guidance from start to finish. And, finally, to his wife, friend, and kindred spirit for thirty-three years, Autumn Alexander Skeen. A writer herself, she was always there with encouragement and an empathetic ear when the words wouldn't flow.

Kelly Black would like to thank Megan Clubb for her clear vision and collaboration from project inception to the finish line. To Mark Kajita, for his support and willingness to share from his formidable financial intellect and his heart. To so many at Baker Boyer who offered words of encouragement—thank you. To Petyr Beck and Thomas P. Skeen, it was an absolute pleasure to work together and to gain from your expertise. And to my favorite project manager, Nathan Black, for troubleshooting, talking workflows, evaluating photo edits, and general cheerleading at any time of the day or night—thank you.

Men gather in front of Baker Boyer circa late 1940s.

PHOTO CREDITS

All images courtesy of Baker Boyer archives except as indicated below.

Front Cover
WCMss066, Box 31, Whitman College and Northwest Archives

Inside Cover
WCMss066, Box 25, Whitman College and Northwest Archives

Back Cover
a: U-B Photo
b: Greg Lehman/U-B Photo
c: Copyright © Richard Duval / DanitaDelimont.com
d: Kelly Black for Baker Boyer

6: Matthew Zimmerman/U-B Photo
8b: WCMss40, Box 1, Whitman College and Northwest Archives
10: Greg Lehman/U-B Photo
11a: Greg Lehman Photography
11b: Andrea Johnson Photography
12a: WCMss040, Box 1, Whitman College and Northwest Archives
12b: WCMss66, Box 25, Whitman College and Northwest Archives
13: Courtesy of Fort Walla Walla Museum, 10.18.17
15: WCMss40, Box 3, Whitman College and Northwest Archives
16a: WCMss40, Box 1, Whitman College and Northwest Archives
16b: WCMss40, Box 1, Whitman College and Northwest Archives
17a: Courtesy of Fort Walla Walla Museum, 80.16.264.RP
17b: Courtesy of Fort Walla Walla Museum, 80.16.262.RP

18: Courtesy of Fort Walla Walla Museum, UK.UK.1328
20: Washington State Library
23b: Kelly Black for Baker Boyer
25a: WCMss288, Box 1, Whitman College and Northwest Archives
25b: WCMss288, Box 1, Whitman College and Northwest Archives
27: *40 Years a Pioneer*, WW Baker
28b: Kelly Black for Baker Boyer
29: Courtesy Megan Clubb
30a: WCMss040, Box 154, Whitman College and Northwest Archives
30b: WCMss040, Box 154, Whitman College and Northwest Archives
31b: WCMss040, Box 154, Whitman College and Northwest Archives
31c: WCMss040, Box 154, Whitman College and Northwest Archives
34: Kelly Black for Baker Boyer
35: Courtesy Megan Clubb
38: Used with permission of Bloomberg L.P., Copyright©2019. All rights reserved.

41: Courtesy Megan Clubb
42: Brittany Nelson
44: Danita Delimont/Alamy Stock Photo
46: John Curry Photography
51a: Courtesy Leslie (Yantis) Brown
51b: Courtesy the *Tri-City Herald*
52: Kelly Black for Baker Boyer
53: Courtesy the *Walla Walla Union-Bulletin*
54: Kelly Black for Baker Boyer
55a: Courtesy Judy Hicks
55b: Courtesy Tricia Agee
57: Colby D. Kuschatka
58: Courtesy Fort Walla Walla Museum
60a: Kelly Black for Baker Boyer
60b: WCMss104, Box 2, Whitman College and Northwest Archives
61: 2003.3.208, Washington State Historical Society
62: Courtesy Fort Walla Walla Museum, 89.99.3
63: WCMss66, Box 25, Whitman College and Northwest Archives
64: Courtesy John Lucarelli and Susie Golden
65: Courtesy John Lucarelli and Susie Golden
66a: Kelly Black for Baker Boyer
66b: WCMss66, Box 25, Whitman College and Northwest Archives
67: WCMss040, Box 95, Whitman College and Northwest Archives
69: Courtesy of Fort Walla Walla Museum
70: WCMss104, Box 2, Whitman College and Northwest Archives
71: WCMss66, Box 25, Whitman College and Northwest Archives (photo taken by Mrs. H. Brodeck for the *Daily Statesman*)
72a: Greg Lehman Photography
72b: Image provided as courtesy of John Deere, Copyright © Deere & Company. All Worldwide Rights Reserved. This material is the property of Deere & Company. All use, alterations and/or reproduction not specifically authorized by Deere & Company is prohibited.
73: Library of Congress
74: Kelly Black for Baker Boyer
75: Courtesy Nathan Rea & Joe Drazan's Bygone Walla Walla Project
76: U-B Photo/Bygone Walla Walla Project
79: Greg Lehman Photography
80: Andrea Johnson Photography
82b: Greg Lehman Photography
83: John Froschauer/U-B Photo

84: John Froschauer/U-B Photo
85: Courtesy L'Ecole No 41
86: Courtesy Gary and Nancy Figgins
87a: Courtesy Gary and Nancy Figgins
87b: Courtesy Gary and Nancy Figgins
87c: Courtesy Norm McKibben
88: Courtesy Norm McKibben
89a: Courtesy Gary and Nancy Figgins
89b: Courtesy Gary and Nancy Figgins
90a: Courtesy Rick Small and Darcey Fugman-Small
90b: Courtesy Rick Small and Darcey Fugman-Small
91a: Courtesy Megan Clubb
91b: Courtesy L'Ecole No 41
92: Kelly Black for Baker Boyer
93: Courtesy Walla Walla Wine Alliance
94: Kelly Black for Baker Boyer
95a: Greg Lehman/U-B Photo
95b: Greg Lehman/U-B Photo
96: Kelly Black for Baker Boyer
97: Sander Olson
98: Greg Lehman/U-B Photo
100: Courtesy Marcus Whitman Hotel
101a: Courtesy Marcus Whitman Hotel
101b: Courtesy Marcus Whitman Hotel
102: 1998.17.12, Washington State Historical Society
103: Joe Drazan's Bygone Walla Walla Project
104: WCMss066, Box 25, Whitman College and Northwest Archives
105a: Courtesy the *Walla Walla Union-Bulletin*
105b: Library of Congress, Public Domain
106a: U-B Photo
106b: Courtesy Rob Robinson
107: Greg Lehman/U-B Photo
108: Joe Drazan's Bygone Walla Walla Project
109: Greg Lehman/U-B Photo
111: Kelly Black for Baker Boyer
112: Kelly Black for Baker Boyer
114a: Greg Lehman/U-B Photo
114b: Matt Banderas Photography
114c: Courtesy of K Vintners
114d: Greg Lehman Photography
115a: Greg Lehman Photography
115b: Greg Lehman Photography
116: Courtesy Fort Walla Walla Museum, UK.209.1
118a: WCA067, Box 16, Whitman College and Northwest Archives
118b: Courtesy Fort Walla Walla Museum, 03.25.187
120: Greg Lehman Photography
121a: WCMss066, Box 32, Whitman College

and Northwest Archives
121b: Courtesy the *Walla Walla Union-Bulletin*
122a: WCA025, Box 12, Whitman College and Northwest Archives
122b: Courtesy Gail Kimball
123a: Kelly Black for Baker Boyer
123b: Kelly Black for Baker Boyer
124: Patrice Gilbert
125: WCMss072, Box 7, Whitman College and Northwest Archives
126a: WCMss072, Box 11, Whitman College and Northwest Archives
126b: Courtesy Walla Walla Symphony
127: Greg Lehman Photography
128: Greg Lehman/U-B Photo
129: Greg Lehman/U-B Photo
130: Jeff Horner/U-B Photo
131a: Kelly Black for Baker Boyer
131b: Joe Drazan's Bygone Walla Walla Project
132: Kelly Black Photography
133: Kelly Black for Baker Boyer
134: Courtesy Walla Walla Community College
136: Army Corps of Engineers
137: Courtesy City of Walla Walla
138: WCMss068, Box 7, Whitman College and Northwest Archives
139a: WCMss66, Box 26, Whitman College and Northwest Archives
139b: WCMss66, Box 26, Whitman College and Northwest Archives
139c: WCMss66, Box 26, Whitman College and Northwest Archives
141: Courtesy Mark Kajita
142a: Kelly Black Photography
142b: janossygergely / Adobe Stock
142c: Eric Hoverson
142d: Kelly Black Photography
143: Courtesy Walla Walla Community College
144: Courtesy Blue Mountain Community Foundation
145: John Anthony/Blue Mountain Action Council
146: Courtesy Jan Darrington
148: Courtesy of Victoria Wright
149: Courtesy of Victoria Wright
151: Doug Crouch
152b: Tri-Cities Photo Booth Co.
153a: Courtesy Thorin Zanger
153c: Tri-Cities Photo Booth Co.
153: (bottom left) Courtesy Providence St. Mary Foundation
159: Courtesy Cathy Allen
160: Doug Crouch

INDEX

Note: Page numbers in *italics* indicate photographs.

The fifth generation of D.S. Baker descendants gather for a photo at the November 1956 open house celebration of the remodeled Baker Boyer lobby.

Front row from left: David Campbell, Craig Campbell, Barbara (Bambi) Campbell Kontos, Paul Schwager, Cathryn (Cathy) Campbell Allen, Catherine Schwager Bryson. Back row from left: Dorsey (Fritz) Baker, Steve Kimball, Susan Campbell Pratt, Krista Baker Burt, Susan Baker, Tom Campbell, Stuart Baker, Ann Schwager Bethel. Not pictured: Fred Kimball, Frank Kimball, and Megan Clubb.